DETROIT

THE SHOOTING SCRIPT

"SCREENWRITER MARK BOAL DELIVERS
A BRACING PORTRAIT OF RACE IN AMERICA THAT'S
EXTREMELY POWERFUL."

Foreword by Mark Boal

In the summer of 2014, I went up to Detroit to meet a man who had been very hard to find. He was called Cleveland Larry Reed, a common enough name, but it had taken a researcher several months to dig up a working telephone number. I left a few messages. When I finally got him on the phone, he wasn't sure he wanted to see me, let alone talk about what happened to him almost 50 years before.

I promised that I wouldn't waste his time, and he eventually let me into his apartment. It looked like Larry, in his mid-60s, hadn't been out in a couple of days, maybe longer. Living alone, not too steady on his feet, he'd fallen a long way from the glamour and ease of his youth, of electrified nights singing and dancing for the fancy crowds at the Fox Theater downtown.

In 1967, Larry was 18 years old and the co-founder of a Motown group called The Dramatics. They were a bunch of friends who had honed their playground songs into a major-league act, touring the country, opening for Aretha Franklin, the Supremes, all the huge Detroit stars. Larry was deeply committed to his music and didn't court trouble with anybody, much less the police. But one summer night, at the Algiers Motel in Detroit's Virginia Park section, he had an encounter with law enforcement that left him permanently wounded—mentally and artistically.

What brought Larry down wasn't a flaw in his character, or a bad decision he made in the heat of a moment, it was shitty luck and racism. At the height of the Detroit riots, when The Dramatics fled from a canceled gig and were trying to find a safe place, Ron Banks, the group's other co-founder, managed to make it home, and would lead The Dramatics to *Billboard* hits in the years to come. By a twist of fate, Larry and some of the others tumbled into the Algiers Motel, where they crossed paths with a police squad that judged them by the color of their skin. The result was a night of terror from which Larry never recovered. Turn left, go home. Turn right, grab a hotel room. What separated success from failure for young black men in the late 1960s was so thin, it was almost impossible to delineate in the moment.

On that muggy summer afternoon in 2014, after spending several hours with Larry, I found a lot to respect and admire. He had, despite everything, persevered in his determination to live as an artist. He now sung for various church choirs. I left his apartment feeling deeply compelled by his story and grieving for the potential that had been robbed from him.

The sort of interaction I had with Larry was unique, as all people are unique, but not entirely new to me. As a reporter and the writer of three scripts set in the real world, I often find true events and real people as my spark and inspiration. When I started *Detroit*, I thought of it as Larry's story—one man who has his voice stolen from him. But as I learned about what happened at the Algiers Motel, and more broadly about what had been going on in the city of Detroit, the cast of characters grew. The five-day rebellion that will forever mark Detroit's history started as a chain reaction, moving from person to person, group to group, until it engulfed 200 city blocks of a dense urban area. I followed the story outward from Larry's own, interviewing firsthand as many participants and witnesses as I could, while bringing other characters to life from newspaper archives, police reports, federal lawsuits, and other contemporaneous accounts. It was a daunting task. You could take almost any person alive in Detroit in 1967 and they'd have a story to tell. At some point, the screenwriter in me has to tell the journalist to put his notebook down.

Larry's story ended up sharing space with that of Melvin Dismukes, played so poignantly by John Boyega, as an African-American security guard stuck on both sides of the racial divide, and the sociopathic racist patrolman, Krauss, a character inspired by the actions and recorded deeds of a Detroit policeman.

Detroit in 1967 was a highly segregated city, its racial boundaries enforced by the police. Young black men, in particular, were subject to routine assaults and humiliations as a means of keeping them in their place, and it was the accumulated anger and frustration from these encounters that exploded during a routine raid of an after-hours club on a hot July night. I thought it was important to show how even small interactions could be loaded with hostile, dehumanizing intent, like a cop grabbing the backside of a young black woman as she's being herded into a van. I drew inspiration from the disturbing trove of news photos, like a famous one of police in riot gear advancing down the street on a "gang" of elegantly dressed grandmothers. Images like that revealed how fear had erased all semblance of civil society.

During the writing of the screenplay, in the summer of 2015, the story and characters took shape in a haunted mood of danger and sudden death, and I found myself working in horror-genre veins, except that in this case, the supernatural element was replaced with the all-too-real terror of racism. At the same time, the emerging narrative had elements of a crime saga, set against the backdrop of a city on fire. Although, in another twist on convention, the perps are the police in this crime tale.

By the time the draft was completed, and passed on to my frequent collaborator, director Kathryn Bigelow, I'd written something quite unlike the singular focus and sole protagonists of *The Hurt Locker* and *Zero Dark Thirty*. The effort to make *Detroit* a mirror of the chaotic times led to an ensemble piece, quickly shifting between characters in a nesting doll of movies within movies, a riot film that gives way to racial horror-crime that switches to a courtroom drama, with several detours along the way into a band's journey, the miseducation of rookie cops, and the adventures of a pair of young women experimenting with sexual freedom. It was, in short, a lot of ground to cover in a single picture. But Kathryn was encouraging, and over the proceeding drafts, we honed the themes and scope, while attempting to keep alive the spirit of a tough and untamed narrative.

The underlying intention, however, was always pretty straightforward: We wanted viewers not so much to watch the story as absorb it like a physical sensation. The script is itself like a volatile crowd, unpredictable and densely populated. The dialogue was a constantly looming creative challenge. It couldn't live in the past—it had to strike a middle ground between period authenticity and contemporary relatability. Most of all, the character arcs themselves had to bend to the reality of what the theorists call racial power structures. To me, that meant letting go of the screenwriter's trusty toolbox and instead of using character to guide the plot—i.e., that character determines fate—embracing a plot in which social forces triumph, continuously and tragically, over individual will.

A word about research and real events: The foundation of the story, rooted as it is in an historical incident, was provided by an ample historical record, documents, police files, and a research team I commissioned, led by veteran investigative journalist David Zeman, who guided a Pulitzer Prize-winning series for the *Detroit Free Press*, among many other career highlights. The great journalist John Hersey wrote a book called *The Algiers Motel Incident*, which was published in 1968, before the dust had settled. Wherever possible, I took scenes and dialogue directly from contemporaneous accounts, like a newspaper story of a grieving mother on courthouse steps addressing the acquittal of the men charged with killing her son. There is, of course, a lot that is unknown or disputed, and in those cases, I employed poetic license, under a self-imposed rule to never stray from what I understood to be the underlying truth of a scene or an event.

This script is built on a sturdy base of journalism and history, but it is not the same as journalism or history, nor does it aspire to be. As a screenwriter, I take the responsibility of being the creator of a tale, of transforming these raw materials into a drama.

I chose this story from the '60s in part because the decade evokes such lively and contradictory associations. The summer of 1967 witnessed two of the worst civil disturbances in American history—first Newark, then Detroit. It is troubling even now to watch the news coverage of all that violence and destruction, but make no mistake about it—this was an uprising, a rebellion. This was black America lashing out against an entrenched culture of repression and bigotry. And yet the far more widely remembered (and celebrated) spectacle of rebellion from that same moment in time is of the Summer of Love, all those hippies, mostly white, joyfully grooving out in San Francisco. By now, the love-potion stuff has run its course, diffused into little more than an advertising trope, but the events in Detroit are hard evidence of a cultural crisis that remains unresolved, of two Americas that still don't know quite how to deal with each other.

When *Detroit* came out this summer, we had just witnessed the resurgence of white-supremacist agitation in Charlottesville. Sensing an opportunity for the movie to be part of the political conversation, I flew to Washington, D.C., to try and get President Trump to see it. On NBC's *Meet the Press*, I issued my invitation. Chuck Todd asked me if I'd screen the movie for the White House. Yes, I said. "Trump should see it. Maybe he'll learn something."

The administration never called. Maybe Trump wasn't in the mood for a serious movie. I can't really blame him there. It wasn't exactly summer blockbuster material. In any case, I never got my tweet.

A couple of months later, in the fall, I got a clearer understanding of why. After a large group of NFL players decided to kneel during the National Anthem as a protest against police brutality, a Reuters poll found that 63 percent of whites disapproved of the players for this, compared to 17 percent of blacks. The president had no trouble picking a side, aligning himself with the solid majority of white people who remain suspicious, if not outright contemptuous, of attempts by African-Americans to organize and agitate for change. In this respect, we might as well be back in 1967.

In even the best of times, which surely these are not, *Detroit* would have to do a lot of fancy footwork to get past the natural resistance most viewers have to upsetting material. At the risk of stating the obvious, sensations of discomfort in movies are generally viewed much more skeptically than feelings of delight. For this reason, I originally tried to conceive it as a "true crime" story. We all know how that works. We are shown certain facts, then get to play detective, prosecutor, defense attorney, judge, and jury: Gather evidence, construct cases, debate motives and render our own verdicts. The horrors of the criminal act itself are sterilized into hamster pellets for our hungry minds. It's a very addictive pastime.

But ultimately, there was no way to imbue the crimes at the center of *Detroit* with those kinds of genre pleasures. Three young men are murdered and there is no compensating turn in the narrative, and there never will be. Instead, under Bigelow's bravely blunt direction, the tragedy is shown unadorned. Nothing softens the blows. Unusually for a contemporary motion picture, the film asks the viewer to experience the same loss of dignity as the real-life victims. And depending on your own politics and tolerances, that's either asking way too much, or it's an act of empathy with moral implications, perhaps long overdue.

Mark Boal
August 2017

DETROIT

By Mark Boal

OVER BLACK:

A tired voice:

                    OFFICER JIM (O.S.)
               (radio)
          Alright Frank. Proceed.

FADE IN - DETROIT - NIGHT - SUMMER OF '67

Concrete and shadow. Cars moving. People slip in and out
of view.

Above, street lamps burn. But there is still more darkness
than light.

Find JIM with his radio leaning against a building. You can
just tell from his sunken posture that the guy is bored,
bored of his job, bored of being a white undercover vice cop
in this African American neighborhood.

                    OFFICER JIM
               (into radio)
          Frank?

Finally:

                    OFFICER FRANK (O.S.)
               (over radio)
          Yeah

                    OFFICER JIM
               (into radio)
          Jesus Christ, proceed.

                    OFFICER FRANK (O.S.)
               (over radio)
          Okay.

Jim grabs a cigarette, peels off a match, off the flame -

AROUND THE CORNER:

FRANK, an African American vice cop who is also in plain
clothes, plus two white UNIFORMED COPS, hustle through the
neighborhood -- passing RESIDENTS out on their front stoops.
Hostile looks between police and residents.

INT. AFTER HOURS DRINKING CLUB - AKA BLIND PIG - STAIRCASE

POLICE running up a flight of stairs, towards the SOUNDS of
a party.

TOP OF STAIRCASE

An entry door guarded by a heavy-set BOUNCER in a tuxedo.
He ignores Frank and the other cops, folds his thick arms.

>   BOUNCER
>   Private party.

>   OFFICER FRANK
>   Pick another card.

The bouncer shrugs. Frank tries the door. Locked.

>   OFFICER FRANK (CONT'D)
>   I see what you mean.

He drives with his shoulder, splintering the mortise, and
the officers barge in and find -

INT. AFTER HOURS DRINKING CLUB - MAIN ROOM

Casual joint with a relaxed vibe, couches and card tables,
booze, dice, well-dressed patrons, all African American.

>   OFFICER FRANK
>   (shouting)
>   Party's over folks!

Complaints and protests from the crowd. One of the louder
COMPLAINERS catches Frank's eye.

>   OFFICER FRANK (CONT'D)
>   Get moving.

>   COMPLAINER
>   Or what, pig?

-- QUICKLY, Frank throws a choke hold and drags him into a
back office

OFFICE:

The moment Frank closes the door, both men relax.

>   COMPLAINER/UNDERCOVER COP
>   The owner split, Frank, I'm sorry
>   that fell through.

Frank sighs.

>   UNDERCOVER COP
>   (a suggestion)
>   But you got outstanding warrants
>   among that crowd. Check the women
>   too. You lazy.

Frank grabs a lamp off the desk.

                              FRANK
                    Cover your eyes -

Frank smashes the lamp on the table, a terrific noise --

BAR:

Patrons react to the crashing noise -- *somebody getting their ass kicked.*

EXT. AFTER HOURS DRINKING CLUB - REAR - EXIT DOOR

Jim and another OFFICER are attempting to snap a padlock and chain securing a fire exit.

                              OFFICER JIM
                         (straining with the
                          crow bar)
                    Fuck me.

                              OFFICER
                    I'll get a blow torch from the
                    station.

                              OFFICER JIM
                    No that's an hour trip. We'll use
                    the front door.

                              OFFICER
                    Take 'em out in public?

INT./EXT. AFTER HOURS DRINKING CLUB - 12TH STREET AND
CLAIRMOUNT

Blur of nice clothes and faces, young and old moving quickly by, as the crowd of black REVELERS hurries down a staircase under the watchful eye of a WHITE COP wielding a baton.

                              POLICE OFFICER
                    Outside, everyone.

TITLE OVER: **DETROIT. JULY 23, 1967**

As they hit the street, we see that among the crowd are two VIETNAM VETERANS still in uniforms adorned with combat medals.

                              PARTY GOER
                    Welcome home.

                              VETERAN
                    Yes sir.

His war buddy looks out at the familiar scene: flashing police lights, gathering CROWD of onlookers. *Some things never change.*

EXT. 12TH STREET AND CLAIRMOUNT - CONTINUOUS

Up the street, revelers are pushed into paddy wagons as Frank
and Jim confer about the change of plans.

                    OFFICER JIM
          We had to use the front door. Make
          a public display.

                    OFFICER FRANK
          I almost feel bad.

A well heeled BLACK PATRON, could be a lawyer or a banker,
approaches the cops.

                    PATRON
          Gentleman, a word?

They nod.

                    PATRON (CONT'D)
          We're celebrating our military
          veterans back from the jungle.

                    OFFICER JIM
          If you don't have any warrants, you
          will be home in a few hours.

                    PATRON
          Arrests for a private gathering,
          that's police overreach, see --

Jim rubs his eyes.

                    OFFICER JIM
          Sir, I'm tired and I'm about to knock
          your fucking teeth out. You got no
          liquor license on this place.

UP THE BLOCK:

Meanwhile, as she's maneuvered by a police officer, a YOUNG
DANCER gets groped - maybe on purpose, maybe by accident -

                    WOMAN
          Hey!

-- Her HUSBAND clocks this in a quiet rage -

It's clear now that the police have a problem because there
are far too many revelers for the available transportation.
And to make matters worse, the CROWD gathering to watch the
public display is increasingly restless, taunting friends,
mocking cops.

One of the guys in the crowd, a teenager named LEON in a
stylish paisley shirt, calls out to one of the party goers -

                    LEON
          Hey Dave! Dave!
             (Dave, filing into
              the wagon shoots him
              a look)
          I told you you was going to get
          busted!

Leon laughs at Dave.

                    LEON (CONT'D)
             (calling after Dave)
          Alcoholic!

As Leon grins at the scene, someone throws a bottle from
across the street. It crashes against a brick wall.

LEON likes the noise.

It gives him an idea.

TITLE OVER: **3:50 AM**

As doors slam and the police cars pull out, the scene slips
into chaos: another bottle is thrown, then another - crashing
against the wall, then breaking the rear window of a police
cruiser.

The POLICE hurry, panicked.

With slamming doors, they leave the neighborhood.

EXT. 12TH STREET AND CLAIRMOUNT - CONTINUOUS

A KID in the crowd of spectators pokes at the splintered
glass of a store front. Just a little push. It breaks.

An older KID smashes the rest, climbs into the store, opens
the front door to the eager crowd. Christmas coming early.

INT. FURNITURE STORE - CONTINUOUS

A GUY attempts to carry a comically large couch out on his
back. Revelers cheer him on.

                                              CUT TO:

EXT. DETROIT - 12TH AND CLAIRMOUNT - AN HOUR LATER

TITLE OVER: **4:50 AM**

Now a symbolic police presence here and a PATROLMAN is walking
down the street through what has become a very large CROWD
(predominantly black but some whites). The cop makes no
attempt to arrest anyone. He merely observes the vibe of
festive anarchy, an edgy carnival that could go either way.

Gleeful faces. Petty theft, grabbing items off shelves.

And then someone somewhere, we don't know who or why,
escalates...

INT. BASEMENT

Fingers on a Zippo.

Lighter fluid poured on a wooden shelf loaded with bottles.

The bottles burst into flame.

INTERCUT:

Historical footage of the early moments of the Detroit unrest.

                                                    CUT TO:

BLACK BOOTS ON THE STREET.

Come up to see ten young white men in uniform, DETROIT CITY
COPS, holding a tense line, armed with shotguns, as a handful
of FIRES blaze from nearby dwellings.

TITLE OVER: **JULY 23, 1967 7:00 AM**

ON OTHER SIDE OF THE STREET:

A strange juxtaposition of contradictory scenes: about twenty-
five PEOPLE are jeering at the cops in the line, clamoring
for justice, protesting, while elsewhere on the street life
continues in a normal way, and passersby en route to work
ignore both the protesters and the police.

One of these workers, a black kid in his late teens,
approaches the line of cops. This is FRED TEMPLE.

                    FRED TEMPLE
          Officer, you gonna make some arrests?

                    COP
          We were told to let it play out. It
          will die down.

                    FRED TEMPLE
          Can I get through? I got work.
                    (MORE)

                    FRED TEMPLE (CONT'D)
               (off the cop's
               skepticism)
          Ford Assembly.

                    COP
          You a janitor?

Fred decides to keep it simple.

                    FRED TEMPLE
               Yes, sir.

The cop jerks his head, 'Go on', and Fred slips past just as -

SHOTS RING OUT!

Everyone scatters -

INT. FORD ASSEMBLY LINE - LATER

Fred, wearing a face shield, crouches inside a steel car
frame, passing a blow torch over the seams. Turns out, he's
a welder.

One of a few black males in the place.

INTERCUT:

Historical footage of the Ford plant until we sense the
complex orchestration and sheer scale of the enterprise.

                                             CUT TO:

EXT. DETROIT - 12TH AND CLAIRMOUNT - LATER

CONGRESSMAN JOHN CONYERS and his brother NATE CONYERS, stand
on the roof of a car, trying to calm another CROWD.

                    REP. JOHN CONYERS
               (into bullhorn)
          Just settle down now!

From the crowd -

                    YOUNG BLACK KID
          Settle yourself!

                    REP. JOHN CONYERS
               (into bullhorn)
          I look blind to you? I know you're
          angry!

For a moment, it looks like Conyers might control the crowd.

                    REP. JOHN CONYERS (CONT'D)
          We got a lotta problems in this city,
          especially with the police. That's
          changing.

                    ANOTHER KID
          Man, bring Stokley Carmichael down
          here! We don't want to hear from
          your ass.

                    REP. JOHN CONYERS
          Messing up your own damn neighborhood
          is not going to solve anything. We
          need to pull together now!

                    ANOTHER KID 2
               (shouting)
          Burn it down!

A bottle smashes at their feet. The politicians look for a
way out.

                    NATE CONYERS
          Come on, John!

                                                  CUT TO:

EXT. DETROIT STREETS - ELSEWHERE

Find a nice CONVERTIBLE GTO with the top down. Inside, a
MOM, young, white and her preteen SON are ogling the spectacle
of the riots unfolding on the street. They see a WOMAN
running out of an appliance store with a TV on her shoulder.

                    SON
          Can I - can I - please Mom get one?

Mom grins why not. Her son dashes out -

                    MOM
          Get an RCA honey!

Off her excitement -

                                                  CUT TO:

EXT. A DETROIT STREET - LATER

Fire trucks arrive, sirens wailing, and FIREMEN unfurl a hose
from a brass reel.

Water sprays into the flames of a burning grocery store.

DOWN THE BLOCK:

A pack of delinquent KIDS muster the courage to throw some
rocks at the firemen.

FIREMEN:

Rocks inbound. They scan the block. The kids are gone.

Then another fireman gets dinged with a pebble. Not a
dangerous blow. A provocation.

The CAPTAIN blows a whistle to retreat.

Off the hose winding backwards into the brass reel.

                                                    CUT TO:

EXT. CAMP GRAYLING - PERIMETER FENCE - 5 PM

Big motors roar to life.

National Guard caravans depart their training facility, in
long lines of TRUCKS, TROOP CARRIERS, and TANKS.

                    T.V. NEWS ANCHOR PRE-LAP
              Five thirty in the evening: Detroit
              Central High School. Where this
              morning children played, the National
              Guard has established temporary
              headquarters.

The VEHICLES turn a corner, headed towards the area around
12th Street.

EXT. DETROIT NEIGHBORHOOD - MOMENTS LATER

Troops on foot patrol, just a sloppy unimpressive bunch of
kids too skinny to fill their uniforms.

                    T.V. NEWS ANCHOR O.S.
              And now on the streets of the East
              Side of America's industrial pride,
              the National Guard is on patrol.

INT./EXT. DETROIT APARTMENT - EUCLID AVENUE

A 4 year-old girl, who history records as TANYA BLANDING, is
watching the riot news on a T.V.

                    T.V. NEWS ANCHOR
              Ready to quell the rioting by force
              if necessary.

Tanya goes over to the window to look at the street. She
parts the blinds and sees an Army tank below.

TANK POV:

The blinds catch the sunlight and shimmer in a way that could
be interpreted as the metallic glint of a weapon.

                    TANK SPOTTER
          Sniper in the window!

The tank fires a .50 caliber shot straight into the window,
killing Tanya instantly.

                                              CUT TO:

BLACK

                    KRAUSS PRE-LAP
          Oh boy, will you look at this?

EXT. DETROIT STREETS - PRE-DAWN

Dim outlines of the city in ruins gradually become visible
before our eyes.

                    KRAUSS PRE-LAP
          It's so sad.

The RUMBLE of a '65 Packard 4-door.

EXT. DETROIT STREETS - JULY 1967

We see the PACKARD clearly now, the big American sedan rolling
past buildings which are burned down to their frames, the
substructures exposed.

                    KRAUSS PRE-LAP
          It's preventable, you know? That's
          the worst part.

On the horizon, fires burn.

                    KRAUSS O.S.
          Look at this!

INT/EXT. PACKARD

                    KRAUSS
          I mean, this looks like 'Nam. You
          believe this is the USA!?

He's in the car with two other young COPS in street clothes.
Shotguns on the dash. Machine gun visible in the back seat.

                              KRAUSS   (CONT'D)
                    We're to blame. Standing by when
                    the trouble started. Now this.

                              FLYNN
                    Uh-huh.

In the passenger seat, that's Krauss's partner, FLYNN -- an
okay guy, wife and whatnot, plays shortstop on the Police
Baseball team. Not the most ambitious fellow in the
department.

                              FLYNN (CONT'D)
                    What can you do... crazy.

Nodding behind them is DEMENS, the third guy on the team
today. He's wired up and looking for a fight.

                              DEMENS
                    Not crazy. They know exactly what
                    they're doing! This is gonna be
                    worse than '43.

                              FLYNN
                    Sure, sure.

                              KRAUSS
                    We gotta stop failing these people!
                    We're letting them down left and
                    right.

EXT./INT PACKARD - CONTINUOUS

They keep driving through the broken city.

All eyes on the street ...

- SUDDENLY

STREET

They spot a teenage LOOTER in a paisley shirt. We recognize
him as Leon from the opening scene at the blind pig.

He's stepping out of a grocery store with two bags of
groceries in his arms

                              KRAUSS
                    Take, for example, this mother
                    fucker right here -

Krauss taps the brakes and **flies out of the car.** Flynn follows
with Krauss while Demens stays back. LEON spots them and
flees.

                              KRAUSS (CONT'D)
            HALT!!

Krauss raises his shotgun and fires -

-- Buckshot strikes Leon *in the back*.

-- He drops one bag of groceries but keeps running, and
Krauss and Flynn give chase.

EXT. ALLEY

Flynn raises a shotgun and fires. It grazes him. And again,
Leon stumbles - drops the GROCERY BAG, beans and canned
pineapple spill out, then keeps running down another alley.

                              FLYNN
            Incredible!

The cops come dashing around the corner as he's climbing a
fence, and they fire yet again. Blood spurts but Leon
keeps in flight, going over the fence, and tumbling out of
sight.
                              FLYNN (CONT'D)
            What a fucking specimen!

Krauss struggles to climb the fence. He's no athlete.

                              FLYNN (CONT'D)
            Forget it, Phil. We're not supposed
            to shoot looters anyway.

Off Krauss's look through the chain link fence -

                                                        CUT TO:

EXT. DETROIT ALLEY - MOMENTS LATER

Leon is badly wounded, weaving down the block.

He crawls under a parked car.

LEON POV: from under the car he can see the tires of other
cars rolling by.

He looks down at his shirt now, sees blood. We stay with
him as traffic and pedestrians flow by.

UP THE BLOCK:

An OLD AFRICAN AMERICAN WOMAN, Southern migrant, scans the
'hood from her front porch. Hard-won dignity in her gaze.
She gets herself upright, then negotiates the porch steps
sideways like a crab, using her cane as an extra leg.

22

PARKED CAR -

LEON, breathing.

OLD LADY -

She hobbles down the street with her cane.

LEON POV -

Her old shoes.

OLD LADY -

She stoops down to his level -

                    OLD LADY
          What are you doing under there?

                    LEON
          I'm just down the street. Please
          get my wife, Roberta. We're on 5th
          street. Roberta.

                    OLD LADY
          You need the ambulance!

                    LEON
          No! No police. Just please go get
          Roberta.

                                        CUT TO:

INT. DISMUKES' HOUSE - AFTERNOON - DETROIT

Sunlight filters through the drawn blinds. DISMUKES is
sleeping when the phone rings. He's a big dude, tall, mid-
twenties, with a determined set to his face. In fact,
everything about his expression suggests that he's going to
make the world work for him.

But the damn phone keeps ringing.

                    DISMUKES
               (picking up the ringing
                phone)
          I'm off - worked a double.
               (beat)
          Alright, alright.

INT. DISMUKES HOUSE - KITCHEN - MOMENTS LATER

                    DISMUKES MOTHER
          Surprised to see you up.

Dismukes, now dressed in a blue security company uniform, addresses a coffee pot and grounds with serious intent. He adjusts the mixture and makes the brew, administers the boiling water, all very precise:

> DISMUKES
> Mister LeFrank called - he wants me to work.

> DISMUKES MOTHER
> I thought Vinny was your boss.

> DISMUKES
> Two jobs, two bosses, ma. The security company needs me for the looting.

> DISMUKES MOTHER
> Looting?

> DISMUKES
> Watch the news, ma.

Dismukes has his coffee now, and he heads towards the living room closet, flicking on the TV on the way.

> DISMUKES (CONT'D)
> (shouting to his mother)
> People are losing their minds.

CLOSET:

In the back behind some clothes he pulls out a .308 Rifle, a pistol, and ammo for both.

TV:

> T.V. NEWS ANCHOR
> Day Three of the Detroit riots showed no signs of slowing down as angry rioters burned buildings to the ground...

> DISMUKES
> Right, burn your own building.

Mom stares at the TV.

> T.V. NEWS ANCHOR
> ...And now we turn for more on this developing story to our police reporter to bring us the perspective of law enforcement.

                    T.V. NEWS REPORTER
          Jim, police here report being attacked
          by snipers...

                    DISMUKES MOTHER
          Snipers?!

He heads to the door, wrapping the rifle in a coat.

                    DISMUKES
          Same thing happened in Newark.

Kissing her good-bye.

                    DISMUKES (CONT'D)
          Don't forget your pills.

                    DIMUKES MOTHER
          I always take my pills!

He smiles, exits.

EXT. DETROIT - DISMUKES' NEIGHBORHOOD

Dismukes makes his way down overcrowded streets, still lively
despite the riots. KIDS playing games. A GIRL and her
BOYFRIEND, necking. FACTORY WORKERS heading to the job, or
coming home. And cars - cars everywhere. DISMUKES is greeted
(or at least acknowledged) by many of the residents.

                    KID
          What's happening, Preacher?

                    DISMUKES
          Work. Money don't come from magic.

The kid is sorry he asked.

                    KID
          That's right.

                    DISMUKES
          Don't just say I'm right. Apply it,
          brother. *Be* right.

The kid nods, wishing this would end. Dismukes keeps going
to his rusty ride.

INT./EXT. DISMUKES JALOPY - CONTINUOUS

He turns the key, puffs of exhaust, and rattles into traffic.

                                        CUT TO:

EXT. DETROIT POLICE STATION HOUSE #10 - EVENING

Krauss, Flynn, and Demens pull up and get out.

The outside of the police station has been militarized with
Jeeps and A DOZEN NATIONAL GUARD SOLDIERS piled around.

INT. DETROIT POLICE STATION HOUSE #10 - CONTINUOUS

COPS shouting racial epithets. Nearly a HUNDRED SUSPECTS in
handcuffs are seated up against the wall, many wounded, all
of them are black.

Krauss and his crew enter and push their way towards a DESK
SERGEANT. (Find the TV playing on the sergeant's desk in
the background) -

                    COP
              (re: his handcuffed
               suspect)
         Where am I supposed to put him?

                    SERGEANT
         I don't care. Take him to your house!

                    KRAUSS
         Sarge.

                    SERGEANT
         Go straight to hell.

For the first time, Krauss seems thrown.

                    KRAUSS
         What Sarge what?

                    SERGEANT
         Homicide detectives wanna word with
         you.

INT. DETECTIVE'S OFFICE - CONTINUOUS

A couple of DETECTIVES stand in the corner as Krauss walks
in with Flynn and Demens.

                    DETECTIVE
         Just him.
              (re: Krauss)

Flynn and Demens hang back.

                    DETECTIVE (CONT'D)
         We got a DOA at Ford Hospital, young
         black, shotgunned in the vicinity of
                    (MORE)

26

                         DETECTIVE (CONT'D)
          Virginia Park. Did I hear on the
          radio - you shoot a black guy earlier?

                         KRAUSS
          Missed. We called it in.

                         DETECTIVE
          You missed?

                         KRAUSS
          Maybe I clipped him. He was real
          fast.

                         DETECTIVE
          You know what we do here?

                         KRAUSS
          Homicide.

                         DETECTIVE
          That's right. We investigate murders.
          Sit down, patrolman.

Krauss sits. The Detective walks out of the room. Off
Krauss's face --

                                              CUT TO:

EXT. DETROIT - OVERHEAD VIEW

                    MARTHA AND THE VANDELLAS PRE-LAP
          "Calling out around the World, are
          you ready for a brand new beat?"

From up here we can see that while part of the city smolders,
other neighborhoods remain normal.

SINGING grows louder.

                    MARTHA AND THE VENDELLAS PRE-LAP
          "Summer's here and the time is right
          for dancing in the streets."

[The Song is "Dancing in the Streets," the '67 Billboard hit
by Martha and the Vandellas]

                                              CUT TO:

EXT. THE FOX PARKING LOT

Nice cars pulling up. Folks dressed to dance.

                    MARTHA AND THE VANDELLAS PRE-LAP
               (singing)
          "They're Dancing in Chicago. Down
          in New Orleans."

INT. THE FOX - MUSIC HALL

The real MARTHA and the VANDELLAS are on stage.

                    MARTHA AND THE VANDELLAS
               (singing)
          Can't forget the Motor City!

The crowd goes wild.

                    MARTHA AND THE VANDELLAS (CONT'D)
          All we need is music, sweet music.

INT. THE FOX - BACKSTAGE

In a hallway backstage, FOUR YOUNG SINGERS dressed in flashy
green, pace around full of nervous energy and stage-fright.

Band leader CLEVELAND LARRY REED - twenty, African American,
a rising young Motown artist - is whispering to himself -

                    LARRY
          It's gonna be good, it's gonna be
          good.

Larry, as we will come to see, is a both an artist and a
wild-card. His mood swings from fits of laughter to bouts
of gloom. He is a child of the streets with plenty of hustle,
but he doesn't court trouble with anyone. He is focused on
his career as a professional musician. His bandmate and
friend, MORRIS, has a more political and social outlook.

                    MORRIS
          You pray. I'll make sure we get
          paid.

                    LARRY
          No, come with me - it's gonna be
          good.

                    MORRIS
          It's gonna be good.

                    LARRY
          Yeah, it's gonna be good.

                    MORRIS
          Okay, brother. We're with you.

                    LARRY
          It's gonna be good.

Larry turns to a third friend, JIMMY, and gives him a look.
Then he nods his head and makes a silent count, one, two...
Three... All the guys together:

                    LARRY, JIMMY, MORRIS:
          It's gonna be good.

                    LARRY
          Alright. Key!

Morris sings a note. Jimmy sings a note, a little off, Larry
shakes his head. He gets it right the second time.

                    MORRIS
          Where's Fred?

                    JIMMY
          He's late.

                    MORRIS
          I can see that, brother.

                    LARRY
          Is the A&R man here?

                    MORRIS
          He's out there waiting to get his
          mind blown.

Larry peeks out of the curtain.

STAGE:

                    MARTHA AND THE VANDELLAS
               (singing)
          "There'll be music everywhere /
          There'll be swingin', swayin' and
          records playin' And dancin' in the
          streets"

AUDIENCE:

One white guy looks particularly groovy in an ORANGE JACKET.

                    MORRIS (O.S.)
          That's him in the orange jacket,
          man.

BACKSTAGE:

Still peeking through the curtain -

                    LARRY
          Oh, man, he's sharp.

                    MORRIS
          He's Motown Records.

Just then, Fred shows up, out of breath.

                    LARRY
          You're late.

                    FRED TEMPLE
          Almost lost my job getting here.
          Ford don't give a shit about Motown.

                    LARRY
          I don't give a shit about the Ford
          Motor Company. Bumper cars and sheet
          metal motherfucker!? You about to
          be with the STARS!

                    FRED TEMPLE
          I need to buy bread, Negro.
               (realizes he doesn't
                want to upset Larry)
          It's gonna be good.

                    LARRY
          Sure?

Fred nods.

                    LARRY (CONT'D)
          Alright. Hand me a towel, man. I'm
          perspiring.

FRED digs into his bag, hands LARRY a towel.

                    LARRY (CONT'D)
          Thanks, brother. I need you here.

                    FRED TEMPLE
          I'm here, man.

Darryl does the one thing that always puts Larry in a good
mood. He sings one of Larry's songs.

                    DARRYL
               (singing)
          Some people are made of plastic -

Joining in -

                    LARRY
               (singing)
          Some people are made of wood -

                    MORRIS
               (singing)
          Some people have hearts of stone -

                    JIMMY
               (singing)
          Some people are up to no good -

               LARRY, JIMMY, DARRYL, MORRIS:
          But baby I'm for real / I'm as real
          as real can get /

The STAGE MANGER comes in and watches them.

               LARRY, JIMMY, DARRYL, MORRIS: (CONT'D)
          If what you're looking for is real
          loving / Then what you see is what
          you get.

                    STAGE MANAGER
          You're next.

                                                  CUT TO:

INT. THE FOX

STAGE:

                    ANNOUNCER
          And our next very special guest, in
          a few minutes, Detroit's own, The
          Dramatics.

Respectful applause from the crowd.

BACKSTAGE:

The boys are delighted.

                    LARRY
          This is it! Move out the way!

But then...

                    LEAD SINGER OF THE VANDELLAS (O.S.)
          Ladies and Gentleman, I have some
          bad news.

STAGE:

                    LEAD SINGER OF THE VANDELLAS
      Oh, come on now, this is Detroit.
      Everyone has to go home is all.
      We'll be back.

From the back of the room -

                    SCARED AUDIENCE MEMBER
      It's the riots!!

The crowd gets restless, scared -

                    LEAD SINGER OF THE VANDELLAS
      The police said there ain't nothing
      to worry about. Just everybody, if
      you don't mind, we're going to -

The crowd starts to lose it -

                    LEAD SINGER OF THE VANDELLAS (CONT'D)
      Stay calm everyone - stay calm -

BACKSTAGE - CONTINUOUS

                    LARRY
      Oh, no. Not today.

                    FRED
      We got to go.

People start rushing past them, heading for the exits. But
Larry stays frozen. Fred starts pushing Larry out of the
backstage area -

                    LARRY
      No.

Larry doubles back, pushes against the tide of stagehands in
the narrow corridor, and makes his way to the stage curtains
and pushes through to -

THE FOX THEATER STAGE

Though the room is empty, it's still magnificent. The gold
leafed splendor of the ceiling. Red carpet and velvet chairs.

Mahogany walls like in European churches.

Larry goes to the microphone.

He touches it delicately.

Looks out at what might have been.

Then he picks up the microphone -

>   LARRY
>   (singing softly into
>   mic)
>   What you see is what you get / What
>   you see is what you get.

It sounds beautiful. The room, acoustically pristine.

Fred appears in the wings.

Larry ignores him.

Then he walks out the front door.

                                        CUT TO:

EXT. DETROIT STREET - NEAR THE FOX THEATER - MOMENTS LATER

Total disorder.

Larry and the band members run to catch a CITY BUS.

                                        CUT TO:

INT. POLICE STATION #10 - HOMICIDE DETECTIVE'S OFFICE

Krauss has been waiting in the office. His eyes are closed,
dozing. The DETECTIVE walks in, waking Krauss.

>   KRAUSS
>   Excuse me. Been working straight
>   shifts since the riot started.

>   DETECTIVE
>   The guy you shot at didn't make it
>   home.

FLASHBACK:

LEON staggering down the street, weaving, bloody -

>   DETECTIVE
>   Ambulance found him bleeding out
>   under a car.

PRESENT:

>   KRAUSS
>   You sure it's the same guy?

                    DETECTIVE
          He's the only Virginia Park shooting
          today. You carry a shotgun, he had
          shotgun wounds. You wanna play
          ballistics?

                    KRAUSS
          Jesus Christ, I'm sorry.

                    DETECTIVE
          That's it?

                    KRAUSS
          What else?

                    DETECTIVE
          You shot him in the back.

                    KRAUSS
          He was running away from me - where
          else was I supposed to shoot?

                    DETECTIVE
          My point was ... him being no threat
          to you.

                    KRAUSS
          In hindsight. But I'm thinking,
          "Why is he running, if all he did
          was steal groceries? Maybe he's
          killed someone in the grocery store."
          He's avoiding the police. What do
          you assume from that?

                    DETECTIVE
          You don't assume -

Beat.

                    DETECTIVE (CONT'D)
          If he had a weapon in his hand, that's
          another story. We don't shoot for
          robbery.

                    KRAUSS
          You know, it's a war zone out there.

Detective keeps writing, then looks up, encouragingly -

                    DETECTIVE
          The 10th had to shut down.

                    KRAUSS
          They're destroying the city.
                    (MORE)

34

                         KRAUSS (CONT'D)
          And we're facilitating by the message
          we send... that it's okay, go ahead,
          burn your houses down, rob stores,
          total chaos. Where does that lead
          to long term, Detective?

                         DETECTIVE
          Alright, kid. Thank you.

                         KRAUSS
          ...Anytime.

                         DETECTIVE
          I'm recommending murder charges.

                         KRAUSS
          ...

                         DETECTIVE
          You go back to work, wait to hear
          from the D.A.

Krauss heads for the door.

                         DETECTIVE (CONT'D)
          Hey kid, calm down out there.

INT. HALLWAY - OUTSIDE THE DETECTIVE'S OFFICE - MOMENTS LATER

Krauss, walking down the hall, is joined by his partners
Flynn and Demens. As they walk out of the police station -

                         DEMENS
          Trouble?

                         KRAUSS
          Forget it.
              (puts Demens in a
               jovial headlock)
          He's just doing his job.

                                               CUT TO:

INT. CITY BUS - LATER

Larry and the band ride the bus - in a different part of
town now - when suddenly a rock comes through the window.

                         MORRIS
          These people rising up!

Larry wants none of it.

                              LARRY
                  We got to get off the street.

EXT. DETROIT STREET - MOMENTS LATER

The Dramatics run down a street until they are stopped by a
line of SOLDIERS facing the other direction against a CROWD
of black people.

They double back. Smoke clouds on the horizon.

EXT. DETROIT SCHOOL STREET - MOMENTS LATER

They duck into a nook in between two buildings

                              DARRYL
                  We need to split up.

                              MORRIS
                  Five brothers together, you know
                  they gonna say we're a gang.

                              LARRY
                  Come on now. We need to rehearse.

                              DARRYL
                  My mother will worry about me -

                              MORRIS
                  Let's go to 12th Street. Be a part
                  of it.

                              LARRY
                  No. We're gonna go to the Algiers,
                  it's right on Woodward, and write
                  some songs. And they got a swimming
                  pool and girls. Get wet two ways.

                              LARRY (CONT'D)
                  We working musicians, right? Let's
                  go then.

- Everyone starts to run again

                              MORRIS
                       (shouting, jokingly
                        imitating Black Power
                        Movement)
                  As-Salam Alaykum, my brother --

EXT. DETROIT STREET - MOMENTS LATER

The band moves on, passing two WHITE COPS who tower over a
BLACK KID squirming on the ground. A baton is raised. They
run.

36

EXT. ALGIERS MOTEL - STREET - LATER

This part of the city has not been touched by the rebellion.
The leafy streets are quiet.

They made it.

INT. ALGIERS MOTEL - MOMENTS LATER

Room keys slide across a desk.

                    MOTEL CLERK
          Eleven dollars a night. Pay in
          advance.

                    LARRY
          Not a problem.
               (tosses down the bills)

                    MOTEL CLERK
          Sign here. To rent a room you need
          to be at least eighteen years old.

Larry tosses bills on the table.

                    LARRY
          Add that up to eighteen.

EXT. ALGIERS MOTEL POOL AREA

The POOL-SIDE scene is hopping - black girls and young guys,
lounging around, listening to music, frolicking in the water
and notably, TWO WHITE GIRLS in the mix. They make their
way to the ANNEX and their room -

INT. ALGIERS MOTEL ROOM

The band crams into the small room.

                    LARRY
          What do you want for eleven dollars?
          Okay - first up, let me hear - "All
          Because of You."

The guys begin to sing -

                    MORRIS
          *Look in my eyes and don't you see
          water -*

                    BAND
          It's all because of you.

EXT. ALGIERS MOTEL POOL AREA - LATER

Ripples in the water of a swimming pool.

A girl dives into the swimming pool - her boyfriend follows
with an awkward cannonball.

> ALL BBAND O.S.
> *It's all because of you*

The song continues as we observe the improvised party scene -
a guy fumbles with a pool toy, joints passed, music played,
dancing, etc - in a quick montage.

The sun goes down.

INT. ALGIERS MOTEL ROOM - MUCH LATER

The boys are now lying on beds and on the floor.

It's been awhile since anyone contributed anything
interesting.

> LARRY
> Somebody. Something.

> JIMMY
> Dig this.

Morris starts humming the melody to STOP IN THE NAME OF LOVE.

> LARRY
> 'Stop In the Name of Love?'

Morris motions for the other band members to keep humming -

> JIMMY
> No man. No. This is different.
> It's a hit.
> (singing now)
> Stop! Fucking-up-our-neighborhood!

Laughs.

> JIMMY (CONT'D)
> (still signing)
> Before we break your ass. Think it
> o-over. Think it o-over.

Darryl rises -

> DARRYL
> (signing)
> Stop!
> (MORE)

                         DARRYL (CONT'D)
                    Trying to make us work all night.
                    Be-cause I wanna go home,
                    La--arry
                    Think it o-over.

                         LARRY
                    Real smart.

Morris stands and makes the call.

                         MORRIS
                    We out man! I can't be in here
                    singing - supposed to be outside
                    swinging.

                         LARRY
                    Okay Malcolm.

Morris slaps his friend's hand -

                         MORRIS
                    Later man.

Larry nods and Morris walks out. The rest of the band
follows. Fred rises too, expecting Larry to go but when he
sees that Larry isn't moving, Fred sits back down.

                                                  CUT TO:

EXT. ALGIERS MOTEL STREET - BY THE GREAT LAKES INSURANCE
BUILDING - EARLY EVENING

A white Detroit City COP is messing with a black KID on the
street corner. Observant viewers will notice the giant
ALGIERS MOTEL sign in the background.

The Cop has a shotgun on the kid.

                         KID
                    I don't have no watch - how am I
                    supposed to know what time it is?

                         COP
                       (pokes him in the
                        mouth with the shotgun)
                    It's past curfew, you know that.
                    Get. Off. My street.

From across the street, Dismukes watches and now crosses
towards the altercation.

                    KID
          You gonna shoot me because I don't
          have a watch?
                (pushing against the
                 shotgun)
          Kill me?

Dismukes is now next to the Cop.

                    DISMUKES
          Lebron get over here-
              (grabbing the kid)
          Dummy -
              (hits him on the side
              of the head. To
              cop:)
          He's my nephew. I'm with United
          Security. I'm guarding that grocery
          over there -

The cop shrugs and goes back towards his car, and we follow
Dismukes as he drags the kid across the street.

                    KID
          I ain't your nephew, motherfucker.

                    DISMUKES
          Move off the street.

                    KID
          They let you out, Uncle Tom -

Dismukes smiles, keeps pushing the kid down the block -

                    KID (CONT'D)
          Push me again, I'll whoop your ass.

                    DISMUKES
          You're not going to kick my ass -

                    KID
          Dumb jacky giant -- I'll bust your
          head to the white meat.

Dismukes doesn't take the bait. He keeps smiling, calm and
relaxed.

                    DISMUKES
          You won't kick my ass.
              (earnestly)
          I'm a black belt in karate...

                    KID
          ...

                    DISMUKES
          And even if you did win, ten guys
          over there -
               (pointing to cops)
          Will be on you, and behind them is
          ten thousand ... Take yourself home.

In the background, a NATIONAL GUARD contingent arrives on
the corner in two JEEPS. Soldiers, led by WARRANT OFFICER
ROBERTS, get out.

                    KID
          So you the cool brother, huh?

Dismukes shrugs. What if he is? He extends his hand.

                    DISMUKES
          Dismukes.

The kid stretches out his hand, too.

                    KID
          Okay, Tom.

Dismukes watches the kid scurry off and then clocks the
arrival of the National Guard.

INT/EXT. GROCERY STORE ACROSS FROM THE ALGIERS MOTEL

Dismukes greets one of his men, SPENCER, an older black guy,
who is sitting behind the front register.

                    DISMUKES
          Did you check all the windows and
          doors?

                    SPENCER
          Fifteen, twenty minutes ago.

Dismukes picks up the house phone, starts dialing, cradling
the phone in his ear as he finishes with Spencer:

                    DISMUKES
          Check it again. I don't even want
          graffiti back there

The telephone line comes alive. We don't hear the other
side of the conversation.

                    DISMUKES (CONT'D)
          Everything is fine. No trouble here.
               (beat)
          I'll sleep when they stop rioting.
          Good night, sir.

41

Dismukes hangs up the phone. Those NATIONAL GUARD troops
across the street look scared as hell.

                    DISMUKES (CONT'D)
               (to Spencer)
          I'm going to go talk to those white
          guys ... Make sure they don't start
          shooting at us.

                    SPENCER
          I'mma stay put, if that's okay.

Dismukes grabs his coffee pot and some mugs -

                    SPENCER (CONT'D)
               (calling after him)
          You sure you wanna tell those white
          boys we're here?

                                             CUT TO:

EXT. ALGIERS MOTEL

Dismukes, in his guard uniform, ambles across the street to
the Guard contingent, carrying his brew. Rifle slung over
his shoulder.

                    DISMUKES
          Melvin Dismukes. National Security,
          guarding the store across the street.
          And I come bearing gifts.

                    ROBERTS
          Thank you.
               (to his group)
          Isn't that nice, boys?

Everyone is very appreciative as Dismukes hands out the cups
and pours coffee.

                    ROBERTS (CONT'D)
               (re: coffee)
          All things considered, this is very
          good.

                    DISMUKES
          Thank you. I don't have my usual
          appliances.

                    NATIONAL GUARD SOLDIER
          It really is good.

42

                         ROBERTS
          Sugar?

Dismukes smiles.

                         DISMUKES
          Don't push it, man.

                         ROBERTS
          It's nice to be in a quiet spot -
          earlier today in Black Bottom we
          took sniper fire. A bullet went
          right here.
                    (motioning by his
                     head)

                         DISMUKES
          Ain't no snipers down here man, just
          you, me and the people partying in
          that motel.

                         ROBERTS
          So in your opinion, how long is this
          going to last?

Dismukes hesitates and another NATIONAL GUARD soldier
interjects -

                         NATIONAL GUARD SOLDIER
          Yeah - how long until ah these
          Negroes...people... quit?

                         NATIONAL GUARD SOLDIER 2
          Yeah - whaddya think?

Dismukes struggles to maintain his smile.

                         DISMUKES
          How the hell should I know?

INT. / EXT. ALGIERS MOTEL

Larry and Fred lie on the two little single beds in their
hotel room, watching TV.

                         FRED
          You'll get back on stage.

                         LARRY
          It's not that simple, brother.

                         FRED
          When they hear you blow? *Money
          raining.*

Larry clings to enthusiasm that he mistrusts.

                    LARRY
          The manager's picky. They don't
          just let anyone on stage at the FOX
          THEATER! And my group don't even
          like to work. See how they left me
          like that?

                    FRED
          Look at me.

Larry looks at his young friend.

                    FRED (CONT'D)
          In the eyes.

                    LARRY
          I'm looking in your eyes.

                    FRED
          You gonna get a record deal.

                    LARRY
          You know what, Fred. It's time to
          fix your little problem

                    FRED
          Ah, man. I'm good.

                    LARRY
          No, no. It's time, my brother

Larry throws his arm over Fred's shoulder and steers him out
of the room

                    LARRY (CONT'D)
          Right now...

                                                  CUT TO:

EXT. ALGIERS MOTEL POOL - CONTINUOUS

Larry steers Fred towards the pool party then notices the
TWO WHITE GIRLS -

                    LARRY
          So they white. Beggars can't choose.

                    FRED
          Ah... man. What does that mean?

44

GIRLS:

The girls, JULIE AND KAREN, just shy of twenty, are trying to plan their next adventure. They notice Fred and Larry trying to sneak peeks.

                    KAREN
          Those boys are eye-balling us.

                    JULIE
               (takes a drag on her
                 cigarette)
          Sweetie, we are broke - there's
          rioting outside - and I'm not writing
          my parents again.

                    KAREN
          Sweetie, you know what I say? Let
          freedom ring.

                    JULIE
          I've had that freedom, thank you
          very much.

                    KAREN
          No you haven't. Freedom doesn't
          mean giving it away for free. That's
          patriarchy.

                    JULIE
          Patriarchy?

                    KAREN
          The one where your thoughts are so
          controlled by men that they even
          tell you what's right and wrong.

                    JULIE
          Only you could make prostitution
          sound high class.

                    KAREN
          We do it together!
               (ironic)
          It's like a co-op.

                    JULIE
          Just do it on your own -

                    KAREN
          I'm not a slut!

Julie laughs.

                        JULIE
              They're coming over.

Larry and Fred approach.

                        LARRY
              Excuse me, Ladies. I'm Larry
              Cleveland. Would you happen to be
              in the middle of a private
              conversation?

                        JULIE
              We must be neighbors, I'm Julie,
              Ohio.

                        KAREN
              Karen, Ohio

                        LARRY
              Cleveland's my last name -

                        JULIE
              And I'm really from Ohio...

Awkward moment.

                        LARRY
              What are ya'll doing in Detroit?

                        KAREN
              Well, Julie here is a professional
              prostitute.

This is lame but Larry gives her the benefit of the doubt.

                        LARRY
              Hmm. Okay.

                        JULIE
              She's kidding. I'm a hairdresser -

                        KAREN
              - And a ho.

                        JULIE
              What do you guys do?

                        LARRY
              I'm a singer in The Dramatics and
              Fred here is my bodyguard.

                        JULIE
              The Dramatics?!

                    LARRY
          Oh yeah.

                    JULIE
          Never heard of them.

Realizing she overstepped.

                    JULIE (CONT'D)
          But I love, love Motown. The Supremes
          are my favorite.

                    LARRY
          If you like the Supremes, you gonna
          love The Dramatics.
                    (breaking into song)
          "Baby, I'm for real / As real as
          real can get!"

                    KAREN
          Oh my God, you can really sing.

Fred beams.

                    LARRY
          It's who I am, you know. I sing.

                    KAREN
          We're going be in show business.
          We're gonna do hair for the Supremes.

                    LARRY
          Florence Ballard is a very good friend
          of mine.

                    JULIE
          You know Florence Ballard?

                    LARRY
                    (winking)
          Oh yes, she thinks she's my girlfriend.

Karen stands, which has the effect of putting her dress
cleavage at Larry's eye level.

                    KAREN
          We were just going to get something
          to eat. Would you like to join us?

                    LARRY
               (to Fred)
          You're hungry, right?

The girls rise and walk out, hips swaying. Larry and Fred
walk right behind them.

                                                   CUT TO:

INT. ALGIERS MOTEL - COOPER'S ROOM - LATER

The room door opens and there's Carl Cooper, early twenties,
tough and very street.

                    KAREN
          Hey, Carl! We're starving.

                    CARL COOPER
          Come on in then.

The girls do. Carl raises an eyebrow when he sees Larry and
Fred in the hallway.

                    LARRY
               (brightly)
          Hello.

Carl is pretty sure he'd prefer that the girls had come alone.

                    CARL COOPER
          I'll say it again, come on in.

Larry brushes past Carl, not about to be intimidated.

He looks around the room - hot dogs frying in a pan - music
from three different radios, all playing at once, SOUNDS
OVERLAPPING - and even worse all Cooper's friends, Aubrey,
Lee, and Clark, are TALKING over the damn music.

These are not Larry's people.

                    LARRY
          Nice joint.

                    AUBREY
          Sit down, man.

Larry sits on one of the beds. The girls are over by the
frying pan, checking out the hot dogs. Awkward smiles and
nods between Larry and Fred and Aubrey, Lee and Clark.

                    AUBREY (CONT'D)
               (re: Larry's clothes)
          Nice duds.

Fuck you, too.

                    LARRY
          We were performing today.

                              AUBREY
                   Uh-huh. Cool.

Larry pats the bed he's sitting on, motioning for Karen to
come over -

                              LARRY
                   Hey Karen, the air conditioner is
                   stronger here.

She sees right through but climbs on the bed anyway. Larry
reaches over and strokes her hair. He leans in and kisses
her. They kiss for a while, everyone else watching them.

                              KAREN
                   (genuine)
                   That's nice.

Larry looks around to make sure the other guys get his point.
Then he motions for Fred to sit down next to Karen. Aubrey
and Lee struggle to find something less lame than a stare.

                              LEE
                   Aubrey, man, turn up the fucking radio.

Aubrey does.

Larry and Karen go back to petting.

Aubrey turns up the radio even louder.

It's obnoxious now.

LARRY gets up and turns down two of the radios, leaving the
JAZZ station playing the Coltrane Quartet *"I want to talk
about you."*

                              LARRY
                   (throwing down)
                   At least let Trane speak -

Now Carl is pretty sure he's going to have to kick this guy's
ass. But everyone quiets down, and they listen as Coltrane
begins a solo.

Sheets of sound.

Then the drums take over -

                              JULIE
                   Beautiful! So sad that he died - he
                   was young, right?

[NB: Coltrane died unexpectedly on July 17 of that year,
five days prior to the riots.]

                                                                49

                    CARL COOPER
          Forty - but he used his years. He
          lived.

                    LARRY
          Unfortunately, it was his heroin.

                    CARL COOPER
          Trane didn't overdose.

                    LARRY
          I didn't say *overdosed*. But John
          Coltrane was a junkie for years.
          Love Supreme? Trane was on dope.
          That don't take nothing away from
          him as a spiritual example. He is
          one of my Saints. But heroin made
          him sick in his liver.

                    LEE
          I heard the FBI poisoned him

                    LARRY
          You wondering how I know? Trane's
          wife is a Detroit musician. Same
          set as me.

                    CARL COOPER
          So you the expert on Coltrane.

CU TV NEWS: "We interrupt this bulletin to bring you
continuing news of the racial disturbances in Detroit. The
National Guard has been called in, and more than seven
thousand have been arrested, most of them Negroes."

                    KAREN
          Why is everything always violent?

Cooper sees a chance to regain his standing with the girls.

                    COOPER
          What about your revolution, from the
          English? There was nothing non-
          violent about that. Liberty or death.

                    LARRY
          She's from Cleveland, man. I highly
          doubt she follows your logic.

Last straw. Cooper pulls out a PISTOL from under his bed.

                    COOPER
          Maybe this will help. Check this
          out -
                         (MORE)

50

                    COOPER (CONT'D)
               (showing off the pistol)
          You white. The police don't mess
          with you. But when you're black
                    (he points the pistol
                     right at Larry)
          It's like having a gun pointed right
          at you. Unless you an Uncle-Tom-
          hankerchief-head.

Larry doesn't flinch. He knows the ghetto games.

                    COOPER (CONT'D)
          It's like this.
                    (play acting, to LEE)
          Hey boy, get over here.

                    LEE
               (playing along)
          What did I do wrong, Officer?

Raising the pistol -

                    COOPER
          You're on my street ain't you, nigga?
               (to Karen)
          That's how they express themselves.
          My street. *My* city.

Cooper cocks the trigger

                    LEE
          Careful man -

                    COOPER
          Boy, I'mma blow your face off!!!
          Step away.

BOOM!

The gun goes off -

- Lee falls back, clutching his chest.

                    JULIE
          Oh my God!
               (rushing over to LEE)
          You shot him!!

Lee rolls over, gasping for breath ... struggles to speak
... at last:

                    LEE
               (faintly)
          Hot dog please ...

Lee quits faking it, gets up, and all the tough guys laugh.
We realize now looking at the pistol that it is merely a cap
gun.

                    COOPER
          Its not a real gun. It's a starter
          pistol, you know, for racing.
          Harmless.

As she walks out of the room -

                    COOPER (CONT'D)
          It happens like that, sister. Just
          demonstrating white power.

Karen gets up to leave, too.

                    KAREN
          So am I, honey.

Larry and Fred follow the girls.

INT. ALGIERS MOTEL - HALLWAY

                    KAREN
          Sorry, Larry. They're usually nice
          guys.

                    LARRY
          Don't let those fools bother you.
          Let's go down to my room and relax.

                    KAREN
          Maybe later. We have to meet another
          friend.

                    LARRY
          Yeah. Find me later.

Off his disappointment -

INT. ALGIERS MOTEL - CARL'S ROOM

Lee and Aubrey are still hanging out, smoking cigarettes,
but the mood is now charged. Carl needs an outlet. He's
leaning out the window, aiming his toy pistol at the
contingent of National Guard soldiers and Dismukes.

                    CARL COOPER
          I'm gonna teach these pigs a lesson
          right now.

                    LEE
          They will shoot you back, brother.

                         CARL COOPER
          Nah.

                         LEE
          Bad idea.

                         CARL COOPER
          They don't know where its coming
          from. Ready. One. Two.

                         LEE
          Carl, relax. It's crazy enough in
          here already.

But Carl can't relax.

                         CARL COOPER
          What?

                         LEE
          We going get our asses beat, man.

Carl smirks. He pushes the gun out the window again, not
aiming it, still looking at Lee.

                         CARL COOPER
          These cops need to learn they can't
          be messing with us all the time.
          Two. Three!

Carl fires off a few shots out the window - bang, bang

STREET:

INSTANTLY - police car tires spinning, cloud of burning rubber -

ROOM:

Carl and Lee laugh their asses off at the retreating vehicle.
Exuberant, Carl turns to his friends.

                         CARL COOPER
          Run, cracker!

                                                  CUT TO:

EXT. DETROIT STREET - NATIONAL GUARD STAGING AREA

An OFFICER turns to one of his soldiers:

                         OFFICER
                You hear that? Shots fired!

The soldier radios it in "shots fired, etc"

Everyone scrambles -

                                           CUT TO:

INT. LARRY'S ROOM

Larry, relaxing on the bed, is on the phone with one of his
girlfriends, LINDA TUCKER.

                         LARRY
                    (into phone)
                Did you hear those gunshots, baby?

                         LINDA TUCKER
                    (over phone)
                I didn't hear anything.

                         LARRY
                Well, anyway ... if I get a record
                deal, we gonna drive a Cadillac.
                    (beat)
                My boy Fred was just telling me that
                the rioting is getting so bad even
                Ford might shut down assembly.

                         LINDA TUCKER O.S.
                    (over phone)
                That's terrible

                         LARRY
                    (into phone)
                It is. But we should make the best
                of it. In a time of hate, love
                becomes more important. Maybe the
                most important. You know what I'm
                saying?

                                           CUT TO:

INT. LINDA TUCKER'S HOUSE - CONTINUOUS

Linda, in her teens, cradles the phone.

                         LINDA TUCKER
                My mom says I can't leave the house
                right now. But I want to ...

INT. ALGIERS MOTEL FIRST FLOOR - LARRY'S ROOM

> LARRY
> (into phone)
> Your mama, right, right. Tell her
> there's a swimming pool over here.

CUT TO:

EXT. STREET - INSURANCE BUILDING NEAR THE ALGIERS

National Guard SOLDIERS taking cover behind cars, scanning
the area with their rifles.

Dismukes is among the crowd of soldiers. He sees Roberts
crouching low behind a car across the street.

> DISMUKES
> Who's shooting?

Roberts has no clue.

> ROBERTS
> From down there, maybe.
> (pointing down the
> street)

DISMUKES P.O.V:

- Checking vantage points from down the street

- Lots of places for a sniper to hide.

> DISMUKES
> Could be any one of those buildings.

POP, POP. Two more shots fired.

> ROBERTS
> Get DOWN!

They all crouch -

> ROBERTS (CONT'D)
> Shoot the lights!

Dismukes ducks back inside the grocery store.

INT. GROCERY STORE - CONTINUOUS

Sees Spencer -

> DISMUKES
> Sniper out there!

Spencer reaches under the cash register and pulls out a shotgun, which he hands to Dismukes, and a second gun which he keeps for himself - and they head outside

EXT. STREET NEXT TO ALGIERS - MOMENTS LATER

Dismukes and Spencer walk through the dark alley.

                    DISMUKES
          Let's find this motherfucker.

                                        CUT TO:

EXT. GREAT LAKES INSURANCE BUILDING NEXT TO ALGIERS - CONTINUOUS

Dismukes and his guy round the corner and find Roberts again.

More shots in the distance -

EVERYONE IS ON THE EDGE OF PANIC.

One of ROBERTS's guys falls to the ground -

                    ROBERTS
               (to his fallen comrade)
          Mike?!

                    MIKE
          I'm okay! I didn't get hit!

                    ROBERTS
               (scared and addressing
                nobody in particular)
          We called the police.

They stayed glued.

Quiet but the THRUM of the city in the background.

And then headlight GLARE as a police car and THREE ARMY JEEPS pull up, disgorging a DOZEN NATIONAL GUARD SOLDIERS and THREE DETROIT POLICE - who just happen to be Krauss, Flynn and Demens.

INT. ALGIERS MOTEL - THIRD FLOOR - ROOM 6

Carl sees all the cars.

                    CARL
          There's a lot of cops out there.

>   LEE
>   They lost?
>
>   CLARK
>   I don't think so. They coming for
>   us now man!

POW POW!!! The window is shot out.

>   LEE
>   Get down, get down!

They hit the floor as the room gets torn to shreds by incoming
rounds.

INT. ALGIERS MOTEL FIRST FLOOR - LARRY'S ROOM

Larry still on the phone with LINDA TUCKER.

- GLASS SHATTERS

>   LARRY
>   What the??!!
>   (into phone)
>   Did you hear that? Window just broke!

FRED looks at him -

>   LINDA TUCKER
>   (over phone)
>   Somebody's shooting?

>   LARRY
>   (into phone)
>   Hold on, baby. I'mma put the phone
>   down. I better get dressed haha.

He puts the phone on the bed and goes for his pants and shirt

THEN -

A BARRAGE OF BULLETS HITS THE ROOM -

- FURNITURE SPLINTERING.

- WALLS CRACKING.

>   FRED
>   What the hell!

- THE BOYS HIT THE FLOOR, HUG THE FLOORBOARDS.

CRACK CRACK - MORE SHOTS -

- THE ROOM IS DESTROYED BY BULLETS

EXT. MOTEL - CONTINUOUS

The combined force of POLICE, PRIVATE SECURITY and NATIONAL
GUARD is arrayed outside, taking cover behind cars and
buildings.

DISMUKES:

He's eager to do something real. Smoke curling out of his
shotgun barrel.

He looks over to the police and sees Krauss, who is also
deadly serious. They connect.

INT. ALGIERS MOTEL - COOPER'S ROOM - THIRD FLOOR

The shooting has stopped.

Carl and Lee look at each in shock.

                                                    CUT TO:

EXT. ALGIERS MOTEL STREET - CONTINUOUS

Krauss crouched low and advancing, Demens and Flynn right
behind him.

                                                    CUT TO:

EXT. ALGIERS MOTEL FRONT DOOR - MOMENTS LATER   *

A line of Detroit COPS including Krauss stacks up against
the front door. One of the COPS tries the door handle, finds
it locked and SHOOTS out the door.

They rush inside, Krauss now in the lead -

INT. ALGIERS MOTEL FIRST FLOOR HALLWAY

Carl comes running down the stairs from the second floor,
hits the landing, sees the COPS, too late.

Krauss fires, killing him.

While the other COPS rush ahead, Krauss hangs back, hovering
over Cooper's body.

He kneels down and places a SHINY OBJECT under Cooper's hand.

It's a knife.

                                                    CUT TO:

58

INT. ALGIERS MOTEL FIRST FLOOR - LARRY'S ROOM - CONTINUOUS

Lying on the floor of the room are LARRY and FRED.

                    COP
          Police!

Several COPS rush in and ferociously attack Larry and Fred -
tossing them against the wall -

The phone is still dangling on the bed, with LINDA TUCKER on
the other line.

                                        CUT TO:

EXT. ALGIERS

Dismukes trying to be stealthy. He's around the back of the
motel. Finds a window to crawl through as the sounds of
SHOUTING and more SHOOTING echo through the neighborhood.

INT. ALGIERS MOTEL - FIRST FLOOR REAR WINDOW

Dismukes makes it through the window and into the hallway.
He hears more GUNSHOTS inside the hotel and cautiously makes
his way towards the noise.

INT. ALGIERS MOTEL - FIRST FLOOR ROOM 3

Dismukes turns a corner to arrive at ROOM 3 - the door to
which is open. He peers inside, shotgun at the ready.

                    DISMUKES
          Hands up!

The room is empty, a messed up bed - Dismukes looks around -

Moves on to the HALLWAY -

                                        CUT TO:

INT. LINDA TUCKER'S HOUSE - MOMENTS LATER

                    LINDA TUCKER
              (into phone)
          Larry?

She hangs up. Dials the switchboard of the Algiers Motel.

                    OPERATIOR
              (over phone)
          Algiers Motel operator, how may I
          help you?

                    LINDA TUCKER
                  (into phone)
              Miss, is something going on over
              there?

INT. ALGIERS MOTEL - FRONT OFFICE

                    OPERATIOR
                  (into phone)
              Who am I speaking to?

                    LINDA TUCKER
              My name is Linda Tucker and I was
              just talking to my boyfriend, Larry
              Reed, he's staying in ROOM A-1 and
              it sounds like someone is shooting
              in there.

                    OPERATIOR
              I doubt that! Hold the line please
              ... I'll check.

INT. ALGIERS MOTEL FIRST FLOOR - ROOM 2

Dismukes comes across Carl's perforated body.

Blood pooling.

Dismukes stares, trying to reconstruct the shooting.

                                            CUT TO:

INT. ALGIERS MOTEL - SECOND FLOOR ROOM 4

OUTSIDE THE ROOM:

                    FLYNN
              POLICE! Put your hands up!

                    GREENE O.S.
              We already did it! Don't shoot!

INSIDE:

Flynn and Demens bust into a room which is now occupied by
Karen and Julie and a black guy who we will come to know is
GREENE, late 20s, a war veteran, older than the rest of the
crowd and already world-weary.

All of them are sitting on the bed with their hands up in
the air.

60

Demens isn't quite sure how to react. He's never seen white
girls on a bed with a black male, let alone an interracial
couple before.

Flynn makes no effort to hide his disgust. Without warning
of any kind, he fires his shotgun twice -- striking the
BATHROOM door in the back of the room.

                    FLYNN
          (casually, re: the bathroom)
        Is anybody in there?

                    GREENE
        No, sir.

Several other COPS now burst in, breaking the weird spell of
the moment.

Flynn clubs Greene with his SHOTGUN.

                    FLYNN
        GET UP!

Another COP grabs the two girls and roughs them up -

                    COP
        What the hell are you doing here?

Julie's head takes a blow - cut bursts open - as the COPS
push them out and Flynn takes a long look at Karen's bare
legs, swishing beneath her mini-skirt.

INT. ALGIERS MOTEL SECOND FLOOR HALLWAY - CONTINUOUS

A lot of frightened bodies crammed into tight quarters.
Here is where many of the historic events of the evening
will unfold. The city cops are lining up everyone, eight
people in all, forcing them to face the wall, spread their
legs, hands over their heads.

IN THE ROOM AT THE END OF THE HALL:

Dismukes is still standing over the body of Carl Cooper,
when Krauss comes up.

                    DISMUKES
        What happened?

                    KRAUSS
        Fella here had a knife and he went
        for my gun.

One of the COPS gets Krauss's drift and -

                    COP
          I heard someone shout "get off my
          gun."

                    KRAUSS
          It happened fast.

Dismukes barely believes what he's about to say:

                    DISMUKES
          I guess you had to defend yourself.

                    KRAUSS
          He might be the shooter.

Krauss looks through Carl's wallet, reads his I.D.

                    KRAUSS (CONT'D)
          Shame. Young kid like that.

The blood from COOPER's body is now oozing towards the
hallway, so we swing back there ...

HALLWAY

We are with Aubrey - he fixes his eyes on the floor -- when
he sees the BLOOD.

                    LEE
          Don't look.

Aubrey can't help himself.

                    LEE (CONT'D)
          Aubrey!

AUBREY:

Turns the corner and sees Cooper's body and bullet wounds.

                    AUBREY
          Carl.

A NATIONAL GUARD SOLDIER pushes Aubrey back in line - as
Krauss watches him leave with an evaluative stare.

Aubrey doesn't know it right now, but he should never have
gone to look at that body.

WALL:

Aubrey pins his hands to the wall.

62

                         AUBREY
                  (whispering to LEE)
            They killed Carl-

                          LEE
                    (too loudly)
            No way. You sure?!

                  NATIONAL GUARD SOLDIER
            No talking, you two!

Krauss comes out of the room -

                         KRAUSS
                  (to the hotel guests)
            Terrible news, folks. One of the
            guests is dead. He tried to take a
            police officer's weapon, ended up
            getting shot.

Beat.

                     KRAUSS (CONT'D)
            Carl Cooper.

CRIES up and down the line from Cooper's friends. Larry
gets nauseous. Fred looks at him with concern.

                     KRAUSS (CONT'D)
            May he rest in peace. Amen.

Krauss walks up and down the line.

                     KRAUSS (CONT'D)
            But let's not be stupid in this
            situation. We still have a crime
            scene here and you're all suspects.

Pin-drop silence. Krauss settles behind Fred.

                     KRAUSS (CONT'D)
            Don't turn around. Was Carl the one
            doing the shooting?

Nobody speaks.

                     KRAUSS (CONT'D)
            Somebody better be honest with me.

TWO STATE POLICE descend the stairs.

                        STATE COP
            We looked around - didn't find a
            gun.

                    KRAUSS
               (yelling to State
               police)
          Doesn't mean it's not here!

Then Krauss regains his composure:

                    KRAUSS (CONT'D)
               (to the line up)
          Be reasonable with me. I got nothing
          against you people. Just tell me
          where it is.

                    LEE
               (turns around to face
               Krauss)
          You the one shooting people! Carl
          didn't shoot nobody.

Krauss slams him with the butt of his shotgun and Lee falls.
Flynn drops a knife near Lee.

                    FLYNN
          Pick it up and defend yourself?

Lee disregards the knife.

He rises up.

                    LEE
          I'm not playing your game.

                    FLYNN
          We both know what is going to happen
          anyway.

                    LEE
          Fuck you cracker!

Flynn hits Lee again, prompting Demens to walk out of the
room. Krauss makes a note of his leaving.

                    KRAUSS
          You think you can shoot at innocent
          people and get away with it?

Krauss hits Lee in the back of the head.

Now Dismukes intervenes -

                    DISMUKES
          Let me search the place again - I'll
          take him.
               (gesturing to LEE)

Dismukes grabs Lee and pushes him up the stairs to search
the second floor -

STAIRS:

Lee looks over his shoulder (as he climbs the stairs) and
sees Krauss targeting his next victims:

                    KRAUSS
          Start praying, people. I'm gonna
          kill you one by one until one of you
          tells me what's going on here. I'll
          just assume you're all criminals.
          Which you probably are. If you're
          honest.

Everyone on the line starts praying in an overlapping chorus:

                    AUBREY
          Forgive us our trespasses as we
          forgive those who trespass against
          us.

                    CLARK
               (under his breath)
          Lord let me get this honky in my
          hands.

Krauss misses this.

                    KRAUSS
               (to Larry)
          Pray good and loud.

                    LARRY
          Oh Jesus.
               (louder)
          Please help these police find what
          they need.

                    KRAUSS
          He's really praying!

The TWO STATE POLICE walk out in disgust and we follow them
outside --

EXT. ALGIERS MOTEL STREET - CONTINUOUS

Find Demens outside where there's a crowd of STATE POLICE
and NATIONAL GUARD milling about and we stay with the two
STATE POLICE who had been inside the hotel as they find their
SERGEANT.

                    STATE COP
          I gotta tell you, Detroit PD is going
          nuts in there.

                    STATE POLICE SERGEANT
          Whaddya you mean?

                    STATE COP
          It looks like they're terrorizing
          suspects. Beating and so forth, to
          get a confession.

                    STATE POLICE SERGEANT
          That's not correct. They have civil
          rights.

                    STATE COP
          That's what I'm saying. It don't
          look right to me.

                    STATE POLICE SERGEANT
          Let's give them the case. I don't
          wanna be involved in a mix-up.
               (to his remaining
                officers)
          Let's GO!

The STATE POLICE head towards their cars, leaving the scene
of the crime.

                                              CUT TO:

INT. ALGIERS MOTEL SECOND FLOOR - MOMENTS LATER

Dismukes and Lee search the room with jangled nerves. Lee
looks under the bed - tossing aside sheets and pillows

                    LEE
          They gonna kill us.

                    DISMUKES
          Why? You gonna be crazy?

Lee turns -

                    LEE
          They the ones lost their minds.
          When they saw white girls in the
          same place as black men.

Dismukes tries to rationalize. Not easy.

                    DISMUKES
          They're looking for a *sniper*.

66

                         LEE
              Carl wasn't no sniper.

                         DISMUKES
              So if a guy goes for your gun, you
              gonna let him have it because he's
              black?

They look at each other.

Dismukes shifts his shotgun in his hands.

                         LEE
              You hold a shotgun with two hands.
              Police had a gun just like yours.
              How you gonna even try and take that?

                         DISMUKES
              Lotta ways.

Lee walks past, disgusted. Dismukes catches him.

                         DISMUKES (CONT'D)
              Just don't antagonize these guys.
              Survive the night.

                                                    CUT TO:

INT. ALGIERS MOTEL - FIRST FLOOR

Lee and Dismukes have returned to the first floor where they
find everyone still lined up against the wall.

                         KRAUSS
              Did you find it?

                         DISMUKES
              No. Just this stuff -

Dismukes passes over a couple of knives and an armful of
LOOT , cartons of Cigarettes, cans of FOOD, a CAMERA, a NEW
RADIO.

                         DISMUKES (CONT'D)
              All this looks stolen.

                         KRAUSS
              He wouldn't even tell *you.*
                   (to LEE, grabbing him)
              Come on -

Krauss pushes Lee into a room and Flynn and Demens follows
as does Dismukes.

INT.   ALGIERS MOTEL FIRST FLOOR ROOM 2 - CONTINUOUS

                    KRAUSS
          Lie down on the floor.

Lee reluctantly lies down.

Krauss shoulders his shotgun and draws a REVOLVER, which he
puts near Lee's head and cocks it.

Then Krauss does something strange.

He winks at Dismukes.

                    KRAUSS (CONT'D)
          I got nothing against you people.
          Tell me where the gun is and who
          did the shooting, or I'll kill you.

                    LEE
          I swear I don't know.

                    KRAUSS
          Okay.

And he FIRES.

At the last second adjusting his aim so the bullet goes into
the floor board near Lee's head.

Krauss leans down to Lee's ear.

                    KRAUSS (CONT'D)
          Stay quiet or the next one will be
          for real.

Krauss winks at Dismukes again - sees that Roberts, the young
guy in charge of the NATIONAL GUARD detail, has also witnessed
the mock execution -

                    KRAUSS (CONT'D)
               (to all)
          This is gonna make em talk, watch.

Then he walks out into the -

HALLWAY - CONTINUOUS

Now Krauss addresses the line-up.

                    KRAUSS
          That one didn't even kick.
               (to the SOLDIERS)
          Any of you guys wanna kill one?

The SOLDIERS have varying reactions - some shake their heads, no - but one or two smile at the sadistic display.

Krauss turns to Roberts

                    KRAUSS (CONT'D)
               (to ROBERTS)
          You wanna kill one?

                    ROBERTS
          Sure.

Roberts grabs Clark off the line and pushes him towards the room where Krauss had taken Lee.

                    KRAUSS
          Use another room.

ROBERTS pushes Clark down the HALL to another room.

                    CLARK
          Don't shoot me, officer, I ain't
          done nothing.

                    ROBERTS
          Get going.

                    CLARK
          Please, officer.

Roberts pushes him inside the room.

THE ROOM:

                    CLARK
          Look man, I don't know where the
          fucking gun is. You looked for it.
          Right?

                    ROBERTS
          Kneel Down. And shut your mouth.

Clark gets on his knees

                    CLARK
          Oh man I know you can't murder
          somebody like this. You can't do
          it.

                    ROBERTS
          SHUT THE FUCK UP.

Roberts shoots the wall above Clark - then glares at him.

                         ROBERTS (CONT'D)
              Now be quiet. Or the next one will
              be for real.

Clark nods.

In total shock.

INT. ALGIERS - HALLWAY

Roberts comes back out into the hallway.

                         ROBERTS
                    (announcing to the
                     group)
              I killed that nigger.

Krauss comes up to the girls -

                         KRAUSS
              What's your part in all this? You
              probably do know where the gun is -
              and you're protecting these guys.
              But don't do that. That's foolish.

                         KAREN
              Get away from me.

                         KRAUSS
              You think you get a pass because
              you're white?
                    (to FLYNN)
              Find out what she knows.

Flynn pushes Karen into ROOM 3. She's crying and cursing
him.

INT. ROOM 3

                         FLYNN
              Alright, there. Miss, is everything
              okay? No injuries on you?

He reaches out to her shoulder.

                         KAREN
              Don't touch me.

                         FLYNN
              Try to keep calm. What are you doing,
              living here?

                         KAREN
              It's a hotel. Isn't it?

70

                    FLYNN
          A little prostitution?

                    KAREN
          I'm visiting from Ohio. My father
          is a judge.

                    FLYNN
          Your father know you're here, living
          with the blacks?

                    KAREN
          There are black people here? I didn't
          notice, I'm color blind.

                    FLYNN
          Yeah. What color am I? Blue?

                    KAREN
          You look yellow to me, sir.

He slaps her.

                    FLYNN
          You're working prostitution.

                    KAREN
          No.

He slaps her again.

                    FLYNN
          Fucking these black guys.

                    KAREN
          They're kids. What's the matter
          with you?

He starts walking out.

                    FLYNN
          I'm trying to protect you, miss.
          Stay there.

INT. HALLWAY - CONTINUOUS

                    FLYNN
              (to Krauss)
          She's a hooker, boss.

                    KRAUSS
          Alright.
              (to Greene)
          So you are the pimp.

                                                            71

                         GREENE
          No, sir. You are mistaken.

                         KRAUSS
          What?

                         GREENE
          ...

Krauss grabs Greene and pushes him into the room with Karen.
Flynn follows.

INT. ROOM 3 - CONTINUOUS

                         KRAUSS
                  (to GREENE and the
                  girls)
          We're going to get this straightened
          out.
                  (to GREENE)
          How long you been pimping these young
          girls and destroying their minds and
          bodies?

                         GREENE
          I just met them. I ain't pimping.
          I just got out of the war.

                         KRAUSS
          You're a veteran?

                         GREENE
          Yes, sir.

                         KRAUSS
                  (hitting GREENE, who
                  falls to his knees)
          We don't need pimps in the Army.
          You probably drove a supply truck.

Greene on his knees looks up -

                         GREENE
          I was Airborne.

                                             CUT TO:

INT. ALGIERS MOTEL FIRST FLOOR HALLWAY

Everyone lined up against the wall is temporarily unguarded.
All the COPS are dealing with Greene and the girls.

                         LARRY
                  (whispering to FRED)
          We gotta get the fuck out of here.

                              FRED
               They're right outside that door.

                              LARRY
               Go out the back!

                              FRED
               They'll see us.

More CRIES from the next room.

                              LARRY
               Fuck this.

Larry moves as quietly as he can to the front door - Fred
right behind him -

Through the glass he can see -- A SMALL CROWD of LAW
ENFORCEMENT outside, including DISMUKES and a few NATIONAL
GUARD SOLDIERS.

So he moves back to the wall, resuming the position of his
hands over his head.

                              LARRY (CONT'D)
               We're dead.

                              FRED
               We'll make it.

                              LARRY
               We've seen too much, they're gonna
               have to kill us, right here.

                              FRED
               Be cool, man. They gonna get tired
               of beating.

Larry decides to give it another try - and he bolts away
from the line -

- This time heading towards the kitchen and the BACK DOOR.
Fred follows him.

KITCHEN AREA -

They peer down the hallway - see nobody -

- Then they see a POLICE OFFICER outside.

They're trapped.

- They notice another door, leading to a staircase to the
basement.

- Reluctantly they descend the creaky stairs.

- Down into the dark interior.

BASEMENT

A cobwebbed chamber. They push through the gloom.

- Dripping pipes

- A cat scampers past

The BASEMENT exit passageway has a high-window with a view
to the outside, and the boys pull themselves up to get a
peek.

OUTSIDE:

Nothing but darkness.

Then: a footstep. A **black boot.**

BASEMENT:

The boys drop down from the window.

> LARRY
> (whispering)
> We're dead.

Fred deflates.

> LARRY (CONT'D)
> Come on!

They head back up the stairs, making their way back to the
group.

INT. ALGIERS MOTEL ROOM 3

Back to the girls and Greene, who has been beaten, judging
by the bruises on his face. He's surprisingly self-possessed:

> GREENE
> Can I reach into my pocket for
> identification?

Greene takes out an Army Card and hands it to Krauss.

> GREENE (CONT'D)
> Says right there, *Sergeant First
> Class.* Eight tours. Honorable
> discharge.

                    KRAUSS
          This your girl?

                    GREENE
          Met her just now.

                    KRAUSS
              (to Karen)
          What's his name?

                    KAREN
          I don't know.

                    GREENE
          My name is Karl Greene.

                    KRAUSS
          Nobody asked you.

                    GREENE
          You just said, 'What's his name?'

                    KRAUSS
          I oughta break your neck.

                    GREENE
          Look man, I won't make any trouble -
          but I'm not going to lie down for
          you, neither.

                    KRAUSS
          What are you doing in Detroit?

                    GREENE
          Looking for work like everyone else.

                    KRAUSS
          Get back in the line.

                    GREENE
          Can I have my Government card back?

Krauss returns the card and GREENE leaves, escorted by FLYNN.

                    FLYNN
          I was in the Air Force myself. We
          had blacks living with us in the
          barracks. Wasn't a problem at all.

                                        CUT TO:

INT. ALGIERS MOTEL - ROOM 2

A NATIONAL GUARD soldier kneels down to LEE who is still on
the floor.

                         SOLDIER
               Why don't you get out of here - run
               out the back.

A trick?

                         SOLDIER (CONT'D)
               I mean it, *run*. I don't want you
               getting killed like the others.
               Run. Right now.

Lee bolts out the back door. The NATIONAL GUARD soldier
stands in the doorframe, watches him run.

Lee disappears.

                                                    CUT TO:

INT. ALGIERS MOTEL FIRST FLOOR HALLWAY - MOMENTS LATER

KRAUSS and FLYNN confer about what to do next.

                         FLYNN
               The one who was praying good, he's
               okay. And you can scratch off G.I.
               Joe.

                         KRAUSS
               That leaves that big motherfucker I
               took into the room. I like him for
               it.

INT. ALGIERS MOTEL ROOM 2 - MOMENTS LATER

KRAUSS and FLYNN walk in and see that LEE is gone.

Krauss thinks of how this will look in his report.

                         KRAUSS
               Suspect escaped.

                         FLYNN
               We need another one.

Krauss nods.

                         KRAUSS
               Go back to those girls - they know
               more than they're saying.

KRAUSS and FLYNN go back to the line.

76

LINE:

>   KRAUSS
>   Who wants to go next?

>   FRED
>   (quivering)
>   Officer, can I say something?

>   KRAUSS
>   Go ahead.

>   FRED
>   You might have the wrong house.
>   'Cause nobody we saw was shooting at
>   the police here.

>   KRAUSS
>   It's possible we made a mistake.

Wipes the sweat off his brow.

>   KRAUSS (CONT'D)
>   But I need to know for sure. Can't
>   let a cop-killer get away, can I?

He goes up to Karen.

>   KRAUSS (CONT'D)
>   You want to die now, or watch us
>   kill these others first?

Krauss' face edging closer to Karen's - as if he's going to
bite. Or maybe kiss her.

Karen finally snaps. Hysteria bursting out, she SCREAMS.

>   KAREN
>   AHHHHHHH!

>   CUT TO:

INT. ALGIERS MOTEL - ROOM 4 MOMENTS LATER

Flynn pushes Karen and tries to stop her screaming.

>   FLYNN
>   Shut up!

She won't.

The effect is blood curdling.

It triggers Flynn.

                    FLYNN (CONT'D)
          You wanna cry?
               (shouting)
          I'll give you something to cry about.

Flynn reaches out and rips her dress - tearing it off her
body.

She's naked now.

                    FLYNN (CONT'D)
          I guess you don't have any weapons
          on your person.

                    KRAUSS
               (to the girls)
          Aren't you ashamed of yourselves?

                    KAREN
          You're the one checking out my tits.

                    FLYNN
          You're having sex with niggers.

                    KAREN
          It's 1967, asshole.

                    KRAUSS
          Honestly, you don't mind the Afro-
          sheen in their hair? The way it
          smells?

                    KAREN
          You're on some trip.

Krauss shakes his head. These girls are hopeless.

                    FLYNN
               (to Greene)
          You think you can come in my city
          and pimp out a bunch of young girls?
          Would you try that in Alabama? Or
          wherever you're from?

                    GREENE
          I told you, it wasn't like that.

                    KRAUSS
          Shut up. I don't care if you are in
          the Army. I'll drown all you pimps
          in the river until the city is clean
          again.

Finally, one of the National Guard soldiers, ROBERTS, recovers his sense of decency.

>   ROBERTS
>   (to Krauss)
>   You gonna question them or I'm gonna
>   take them outta here.

>   KRAUSS
>   (turns to Karen,
>   kneels down to her)
>   Hey, doll, you might be a good kid
>   after all. Be straight with me now.
>   Who was shooting at the National
>   Guard out there?

Karen takes a deep breath.

>   KAREN
>   Mister, I didn't see anybody shoot
>   at the National Guard. I would tell
>   you if I had.

>   KRAUSS
>   Really?

>   KAREN
>   You can think I'm a slut if you want -
>   but I was raised right.

He smiles. Believes her.

>   ROBERTS
>   I'll get them outta here.

Roberts lifts Julie up, and takes Karen with his other arm.

>   ROBERTS (CONT'D)
>   (to the girls)
>   Let's get you covered up.

>   CUT TO:

EXT. ALGIERS MOTEL - LATER

Roberts and Dismukes guide Karen and Julie, now wrapped in sheets, and walk them towards the main hotel.

>   KAREN
>   You're fucking murdering those kids!
>   Fuck!

>   ROBERTS
>   No girls -

                    JULIE
                (to Roberts)
          Why don't you stop them?!

                    KAREN
                (to Julie)
          This animal did it too! He shot one
          of them.

                    ROBERTS
          No, girls, girls, they're just scaring
          them. It's an interrogation tactic.
          They're not really killing them.

                    KAREN
          Are you nuts, mister? I saw. Those
          guys are getting murdered in cold
          blood.

They've reached the HOTEL and shuffle inside, going through
the door

INT. ALGIERS MOTEL - MAIN WING

                    ROBERTS
                (going through the
                 door to the hotel)
          It's not real. I didn't shoot and
          neither did the other. It's to get
          those guys to fess up about the
          location of the gun.

                    JULIE
          Who said they even had a gun?

                    ROBERTS
          ...

                    JULIE
          If they did, it was just a toy. It
          wasn't a *real gun*.

OFF Roberts' reaction.

INT. ALGIERS MOTEL - MAIN ROOM - CONTINUOUS

They walk into Karen and Julie's room and Julie finally sees
herself in the mirror, touches the gash on her forehead.

                    ROBERTS
                (to Dismukes)
          Take a look at her head.

                         DISMUKES
              Gonna need stitches. Medical
              attention.

                         KAREN
              Will you take us to the hospital?

Roberts suddenly realizes the repercussions of bringing these
two bloodied girls into the hospital - the inquiries, the
investigations -

                         ROBERTS
              Not tonight. You're better off going
              in the morning, when you're fresh.
                   (he looks at the wound
                    again)
              It won't hurt to get it looked at in
              the morning.

                         DISMUKES
              Sure.

He heads for the door.

                         JULIE
              Are we safe here?

Roberts nods.

                         KAREN
              She means are you going to tell the
              police where we are?

                         ROBERTS
              No.

The men leave.

Julie and Karen fall into each other's arms.

                         KAREN
                   (whispering in her
                    ear)
              We're going to be okay, sweetie.

                         JULIE
              But those boys.

                                                  CUT TO:

INT. ROOM 2 - MOMENTS LATER

Krauss and Flynn confer again.

                         KRAUSS
              Let's get our confession already and
              vacate the premises.

Krauss gets an idea.

                         KRAUSS (CONT'D)
              Demens should do it.

                         DEMENS
              Do what?

Krauss raises his voice so everyone in the line can hear.

                         KRAUSS
              You haven't killed a nigger yet.

                         DEMENS
              I don't know about that.

                         KRAUSS
              Come on! Sure you do.

He slaps Demens on the shoulder again.

                         DEMENS
              Whatever you think.

INT. HALLWAY - CONTINUOUS

Demens goes up to Aubrey, grabs him -

                         DEMENS
              Come with me. I need to ask you
              some questions.

INT. ROOM 5 - CONTINUOUS

DEMENS pushes Aubrey inside the room - using his shotgun as
a poker.

Aubrey raises his hands trying to cover his face -

                         AUBREY
              Please, please. Don't shoot me.

                         DEMENS
              Where's the gun?

                         AUBREY
              I don't know. Please don't shoot
              me.

                         DEMENS
              I've got no cause to shoot you.

                    AUBREY
          Please.

                    DEMENS
          I ain't never shot anybody in my
          life.

BOOM!

He blasts Aubrey in the chest at close range.

BOOM!

He hits him in the shoulder - spinning him.

Aubrey collapses in a heap on the floor.

Demens looks at him, then turns - sees that Roberts witnessed
this - or some of it - from the hallway.

INT. HALLWAY

Demens walks past Roberts, and Flynn, and finds Krauss at
the end of the line.

Krauss grins at him.

                    DEMENS
          So that's done.

                    KRAUSS
          Great. Good job.

                    DEMENS
          Yeah. I didn't think I could, but I
          did it. Boy, I feel funny.

                    KRAUSS
          It's the right thing.
              (beat)
          He'll talk now.

                    DEMENS
              (deeply confused)
          What do you mean?

Krauss doesn't catch his confusion.

Plows ahead -

                    KRAUSS
              (to the line)
          Another one bites the dust.
              (MORE)

                    KRAUSS (CONT'D)
          I bet some of you thought we weren't
          serious. This is Detroit. We don't
          bluff.

Krauss walks up and down the line.

                    KRAUSS (CONT'D)
          Who wants to be next? We still
          haven't found our gun, and we're
          running out of time, people.

No answer. Krauss goes into the room where Demens had just
been. Demens follows.

INT. ROOM - CONTINUOUS

Krauss sees the body of Aubrey.

This wasn't part of the plan.

His voice drops -

                    KRAUSS
          You shot him, Demens.

                    DEMENS
          I got him.

                    KRAUSS
          Jesus, Marty. We didn't shoot the
          other guys. We were just playing
          with them.

                    DEMENS
          Playing what?

                    KRAUSS
          A game to get them talking - scare
          the wits out 'em. You know,
          interrogating tactics.

Demens falls silent.

Stunned.

                    DEMENS
          Jesus.

                    KRAUSS
          So he tried to take your shotgun,
          and you defended yourself. Okay.

                    DEMENS
          Oh Jesus.

                    KRAUSS
                  (sternly)
        Straighten out. He grabbed he went
        for your firearm, you warned him.
        You had to defend yourself. Line of
        duty. Fill in the goddamn details.

Krauss walks out, furious.

Off Demens' sickened face -

INT. ALGIERS HALLWAY - CONTINUOUS

Krauss approaches Flynn.

                    KRAUSS
        Marty shot the guy.

                    FLYNN
        Wow - he did?

                    KRAUSS
        We need to wrap this up and get out
        of here.

Flynn nods, thinking it over -

                    FLYNN
        We don't have a suspect. Arrest all
        of them?

                    KRAUSS
        We need to just get out of here.
        They're not going to say anything if
        they're smart.

Krauss scans the remaining guys in the line-up, focuses in
on Greene.

                    KRAUSS (CONT'D)
                  (to Greene)
        You are free to go. You're not going
        talk about this, right? Ever?

Greene shakes his head, no.

                    KRAUSS (CONT'D)
        'Cause I got your name.

                    GREENE
        I don't have yours - I don't know
        nothing about you.

Krauss chuckles. He leads Greene down the hall to Cooper's
body and points to the corpse -

                    KRAUSS
          What's this here?

                    GREENE
          I don't see nothing.

Krauss slaps him on the shoulder.

                    KRAUSS
          Get going.

Greene exits.

EXT. ALGIERS MOTEL - CONTINUOUS

Greene breathes fresh air.

The STREET is quiet. He heads over to the front OFFICE of
the MOTEL, and we follow him as he goes inside.

INT. ALGIERS MOTEL - FRONT OFFICE - CONTINUOUS

The TELEPHONE OPERATOR and RECEPTIONIST look up at Greene.
He walks over to a chair and sits down in it.

                    GREENE
          How long you ladies working tonight?

                    RECEPTIONIST
          We're here all night.

Greene closes his eyes.

                    GREENE
          I'm going to sleep here then. I'm
          staying in ROOM 4. But I'm going to
          sleep here.

OFF his eyes -

                                             CUT TO:

INT. ALGIERS - HALLWAY

Krauss is closing down the scene.

                    KRAUSS
               (to Larry)
          What would you do if I said run and
          don't come back?

Fred and Larry look at each other.

Larry takes off out of the back door -

                    KRAUSS (CONT'D)
                (to Fred)
        Come here and collect your belongings.

Fred follows Krauss into room 2 - where he sees the DEAD
BODY of Aubrey. Flynn follows them. Krauss now gives Fred
the same test he administered to Greene.

                    KRAUSS (CONT'D)
            Is everything all right?

                    FRED
        ...

                    KRAUSS
        Hello?

                    FRED
            You killed him?

                    KRAUSS
        I don't see anything.

                    FRED
            There's a dead guy right here!

Krauss draws his pistol and shoots Fred three times. Flynn
does the same, both of them killing him.

                                        CUT TO:

EXT. DETROIT STREETS - NIGHT - MOMENTS LATER

Larry is running hard down an alley, and we follow him in
real time as he turns down another alley -

- We stay with him as he avoids COPS and SOLDIERS, the city
a maze of LAW ENFORCEMENT.

- And now he's across an OPEN FIELD

SUDDENLY: WHITE SPOT LIGHTS - square on his face, so bloody
and pulped - the light blinding his eyes.

                    POLICE OFFICER
        Halt!

Larry kneels, preparing for the end ...

WHITE POLICE OFFICERS approach

                    POLICE OFFICER #1
                (concerned)
        Look at this guy!

A second POLICE OFFICER starts to pick up Larry.

                    POLICE OFFICER #2
          Come on, pal. We need to get you to
          the hospital.

They pick up Larry.

He sees these white faces and passes out.

                                              CUT TO:

EXT. ALGIERS MOTEL AREA - NEXT MORNING

Birds in the trees.

Everything seems normal.

INT. ALGIERS MOTEL FRONT OFFICE - MORNING

A door opens, the MOTEL OPERATOR walks in, waking up Greene
in the chair he slept in.

                    GREENE
          Go have a look in the back annex.

He walks out the door.

EXT. ALGIERS MOTEL ANNEX - MOMENTS LATER

The Motel Operator walks towards the Annex building, noticing
the broken glass, the smashed doors.

She opens the front door into the hallway.

Turns into a bedroom -

Sees: BODIES SPLAYED ON THE FLOOR, BLOOD SPLATTERS -

                                              CUT TO:

EXT. DETROIT WATER AND POWER DEPARTMENT GARAGE - MORNING

A sprawling facility, trucks and machines, city workers moving
to and fro. The municipal hive.

INT. DETROIT WATER AND POWER DEPARTMENT GARAGE - CONTINUOUS

RASPING gears. The metal teeth turn - white foreman, PETE,
calling across the room -

                    PETE
          Hey Aubrey!

AUBREY SR, a forty-something African American wearing the
Department of Water and Power uniform, loading boxes on the
other side of the cavernous shop, can't hear over the din.

                    PETE (CONT'D)
               (shouting)
          Aubrey! Phone call.

                    AUBREY SR.
          Say again?!

                    PETE
          You got a phone call from home.

                    AUBREY SR.
          ...

                    PETE
          There's something happened. One of
          your boys is in trouble or got hurt.

They start walking back to the office.

                    AUBREY SR.
          Doggone. I hope it's not Tanner.
          He's always googy-googy.

INT. SANITATION DEPARTMENT OFFICE - MOMENTS LATER

AUBREY SR. Stands with phone in his hand.

                    AUBREY SR.
          Yes?

INT. POLLARD HOUSEHOLD

                    ROBERTA
               (his wife, into phone)
          Well Aubrey, they found Aubrey dead
          this morning at the Algiers hotel.

INT. SANITATION DEPARTMENT OFFICE

                    AUBREY SR.
               (into phone)
          No. No. Aubrey is supposed to be
          home.

EXT. DETROIT NEIGHBORHOOD - AFRICAN AMERICAN AREA

Rows and rows of wooden houses, many in ruins.

INT. POLLARD HOUSEHOLD

Aubrey Sr, his wife Roberta, his mother, MAW, and two of his
sons, sit in the living room, trying to cope. Aubrey Sr is
holding picture of Aubrey Jr.

                    AUBREY SR.
          Maw, what is this? A mistake?

Nobody knows what to say.

                    AUBREY SR. (CONT'D)
          It's got to be a mistake because I
          know Aubrey has more sense than that.

                    MAW
          Well, baby, you never know. Let's
          go see.

INT/EXT. POLLARD HOUSEHOLD - MOMENTS LATER

Aubrey Sr and his mother go outside.

EXT. DETROIT STREET - IN FRONT OF POLLARD HOUSEHOLD

                    MAW
          Where is it - the city morgue? By
          the police station?

                    AUBREY SR.
          Yes, I reckon. Five miles.

EXT. STONE YARD - AFTERNOON - DAYS LATER

A large slab of SANDSTONE, fireplace hearth, is being dragged
across the ground by Dismukes. He goes back to another pile
to move another slab, wiping his brow in the afternoon sun.

Three DETROIT POLICE come through the back and surround
Dismukes.

                                             CUT TO:

INT./EXT. SQUAD CAR - LATER

Driving through the Detroit factory district ...

INT. SQUAD CAR - CONTINUOUS

Dismukes in the back, cops in front. The DRIVER looks at
Dismukes in the mirror.

                    COP DRIVER
          Little detour.

He pulls to the side of the street. The COPS get out and
make a deliberate show of *unlocking* the back seat door nearest
to Dismukes.

>   COP DRIVER (CONT'D)
>   Be right back.

Dismukes watches them go through the rear view mirror. Ahead
of him is an empty street.

STREET:

The COPS smoke.

>   COP DRIVER
>   He gets out, I'm going to plug him
>   in the back.

>   COP
>   Within your rights.

CAR

Dismukes stays put. He closes his eyes.

CLUNK!

The passenger door opens - the DRIVER COP leans in -

>   DRIVER COP
>   I figured you for a runner.

>   DISMUKES
>   Not me. I don't run.

>   CUT TO:

EXT. DETROIT POLICE STATION - LATER

Establishing shot.

INT. DETROIT POLICE STATION - INTERROGATION ROOM - LATER

Dismukes is led into a room with TWO DETECTIVES.

>   DISMUKES
>   I assume this is about what went on
>   at the hotel.

>   DETECTIVE #2
>   Something happen at a hotel?

>   DISMUKES
>   If you don't know, I'll tell you.
>   (MORE)

                    DISMUKES (CONT'D)
          I was doing security by Wisconsin,
          and on Tuesday night, we heard gunfire
          coming from the area by the Algiers.
          That direction.
                    (beat)
          The police came, State Police,
          National Guard. There was a lot of
          shooting and when I went in there -
          three kids had been killed.

                    DETECTIVE #1
          No.

Dismukes starts to cry.

                    DISMUKES
          The blood was fresh. It hadn't
          congealed yet.

                    DETECTIVE #2
          Killed just before you arrived. You
          carry a thirty eight?

Dismukes doesn't answer. The Detective slams the desk.

                    DETECTIVE #1
          A REVOLVER!

                    DISMUKES
          I do have a .38.

                    DETECTIVE #1
          Shoot anyone?

                    DISMUKES
          No.

                    DETECTIVE #2
          Strike anyone?

                    DISMUKES
          Not in the way you mean.

                    DETECTIVE #2
          What do I mean?

                    DISMUKES
          Look fellas, sometimes when there's
          a black guy in a position of authority -
          other blacks might single him out.
          Because I'm not supposed to be able
          to tell them what to do.

                         DETECTIVE #2
          We do these conversations in stages.
          Stage one, witnesses. Stage Two,
          suspects.

                         DETECTIVE #1
          What stage are we in?

Dismukes shrugs.

                         DETECTIVE #2
          You don't know what stage we're in?

                         DETECTIVE #1
          No. Specify for him.

                         DETECTIVE #2
          Oh. We're in Stage 2.
               (to Dismukes)
          You're a suspect.

                         DISMUKES
          It wasn't me. The police -

                         DETECTIVE #2
          Here we go -

                         DISMUKES
          - The police shot those kids.

                         DETECTIVE #1
          How the hell would you know that?
          You weren't inside the building until
          after the shooting stopped, or so
          you just said. So are you lying
          now? Or were you lying a minute
          ago?

INT. DETROIT POLICE STATION - LINE UP ROOM

Dismukes stands in a line of other black suspects. Each man
holds a number. A loudspeaker in the corner of the room
squawks and hisses. Finally it becomes clear -

                         LOUDSPEAKER
          Number four, please step forward.

Dismukes is holding the 4. He steps forward.

BEHIND THE GLASS:

Julie stares at Dismukes.

INT. DETROIT CITY JAIL CELL - LATER

Bars close on Dismukes as he's locked in a cell.

                                        CUT TO:

INT. HOSPITAL - AFTERNOON

Larry lies in bed, covered in bandages. The Dramatics are
here visiting.

                    MORRIS
          Hey Larry, wake up, brother.

Larry's eyes flutter. He looks at them. Can't find words.

                    JIMMY
          You alright, man. It's us.

Morris nods to Fred's brother, EDDIE.

                    EDDIE TEMPLE
          Do you know where Fred is?

Slowly, Larry shakes his head, NO.

                    EDDIE TEMPLE (CONT'D)
          The police are saying Fred is dead.
          But I can't find nobody to tell me
          what's going on.

                    LARRY
          What's going on?

                    DARRYL
          You tell us -

Nobody knows what else to say. The room falls silent. Larry
holds back tears.

                    LARRY
          The police.

Everybody knows what that means.

Morris closes his eyes, starts humming a spiritual -

                    MORRIS
               (humming and singing)
          Hold on
          Hold on

Larry collects himself.

                        LARRY
         You gonna sing - sing one of my songs.

                                              CUT TO:

INT. DETROIT CITY MORGUE - HALLWAY - LATER

Aubrey Sr. is sitting on a bench, talking to DOCTOR NANCY
BREYER. His mother is on another bench, giving him some
space.

In front of them is the DOOR to the MORGUE.

Aubrey Sr. clings to this conversation. If he could sit here
and talk to this lady forever, he might never have to
go through that door.

                        AUBREY SR.
         Oh, he's a character, you know. He
         always wants life up to par. I tell
         him "you've got to give something to
         get something"... But he wants to go
         a long ways.

                        DOCTOR NANCY BREYER
         Sounds like a lovely young man.

                        AUBREY SR.
         Do you have children?

                        DOCTOR NANCY BREYER
         Oh yes, I have three boys. The oldest
         is twelve, then nine, and seven.

                        AUBREY SR.
         So you know how youngsters are.

                        DOCTOR NANCY BREYER
         Oh, boy. The way they communicate -
         grunts and groans. My little cave
         men!

                        AUBREY SR.
         Boys especially. They don't know if
         they want to be slick, you know.

                        DOCTOR NANCY BREYER
         That's right. They're still finding
         out who they are in this life, and
         we have to allow for that.

                        AUBREY SR.
         Uh-huh.

                                                              95

                    DOCTOR NANCY BREYER
          Oh, yes.

                    AUBREY SR.
          Hmm.

                    DOCTOR NANCY BREYER
          Yes. Well. I can see that you want
          to go back there.

                    AUBREY SR.
          Sure.

She stands. He doesn't.

She holds the door open for the morgue.

He can't get off the bench.

                                             CUT TO:

EXT./INT. DETROIT WHITE SUBURB - KRAUSS HOUSE

Little house. Lawn. White fence. A facsimile of the
American dream. Krauss pulls up in his car, goes inside,
takes off his jacket, pops a dinner in the oven, pours a
scotch and settles down in front of the TV.

TV: newscaster saying something about the aftermath of the
riots.

INT. POLICE STATION - AFTERNOON

TITLE OVER: **5 DAYS AFTER THE KILLING**

Krauss, Flynn, and Demens are sitting on a bench in the Police
Station outside the Homicide Detective's Office.

                    KRAUSS
          Just remember what I told you and
          this will blow over. We did nothing
          wrong.

                    DEMENS
          I feel like I gotta say something.

                    KRAUSS
          You made a -

Two cops are walking down the hall. He lowers his voice.

96

                              KRAUSS (CONT'D)
                    (whisper)
               Something that took one minute
               shouldn't define your entire life.
               You made a mistake. Say what you
               need to say and move on.

                              DEMENS
               Alright. Alright.

Krauss turns to Flynn.

                              FLYNN
               You don't need to lecture me. I
               know what to do.

Krauss leans back, satisfied. A HOMICIDE DETECTIVE pokes
his head out of the door, points his finger at Demens -

                              HOMICIDE DETECTIVE
               You first, knucklehead.

Demens gets up and goes into the room. Off the slamming
door -

                                                  CUT TO:

INT. POLICE STATION - LATER

Krauss and Flynn on the bench. Some time has passed. Flynn
is called in. COPS walk up and down the hallway. It's
obvious from the way they ignore Krauss, or whisper about
him as they walk, that he's become a pariah.

INT. POLICE STATION - LATER

The door opens from the Detective's Office. Flynn and Demens
join Krauss on the bench.

                              HOMICIDE DETECTIVE
                    (to Krauss)
               I'll be with you in a few minutes.

Demens stares straight ahead.

                              DEMENS
               Some things were said in there.

                              KRAUSS
               Such as?

                              DEMENS
                    ...

                    KRAUSS
          You motherfucker. You're dead.

Flynn shrugs.

                    KRAUSS (CONT'D)
          You too?

                    FLYNN
          We're all going down.

Krauss gets up and walks down the hall.

INT. POLICE STATION - HALLWAY - CONTINUOUS

We follow him as he walks to the exit -

EXT. POLICE STATION - CONTINUOUS

He gets in the car and starts the motor just as there's a
KNOCK on his window. It's the Homicide Detective.

                    KRAUSS
          I got nothin' to say without my union
          lawyer.

                    HOMICIDE DETECTIVE
          You kidding me, you racist fuck?
          Get out of this car before I break
          your neck.

                                                      CUT TO:

INT. POLICE STATION - HOMICIDE OFFICE - MOMENTS LATER

Krauss sits across the table from two Homicide Detectives.
He's trying to run out the clock.

                    KRAUSS
          I couldn't say for sure who went
          inside the building first, whether
          it was National Guard or State Police.
          There were ... let me see ... five
          or six state police present -

                    HOMICIDE DETECTIVE 1
          We have complete statements from
          your partners. We know you shot
          those kids - so just get to that
          part.

                    KRAUSS
          No, I don't recall doing that.
          Where was I? So it was a multi-agency
          effort to secure the scene.
                    (MORE)

                              KRAUSS (CONT'D)
          We had a number of National Guard
          and State police -

                              HOMICIDE DETECTIVE 2
          You're cruising for a bruising.

                              HOMICIDE DETECTIVE 1
          Bang his head against the table.
          Might help.

                              KRAUSS
          Sorry, guys. I'm trying to be
          thorough. I know this is important.
          You don't want to know the number of
          State Police on the scene?

                              HOMICIDE DETECTIVE 1
          I can't tell if you're stupid or
          smart.

The door opens and DEFENSE ATTORNEY AUERBACH walks in.

                              AUERBACH
              (to Krauss)
          Don't say another word.
              (to Detectives)
          What's the point? Coercive testimony
          will be tossed.

INT./EXT. WARRANT OFFICER ROBERTS HOUSE - MORNING

Roberts (in his bathrobe) opens the front door and grabs the
newspaper. He flips it open - bullets tumble out.

C.U. HEADLINE: ALGIERS MOTEL DEATHS

Roberts looks up and down his street.

                                                      CUT TO:

INT. EXT LARRY'S HOUSE - NIGHT

The Dramatics are gathered outside of Larry's place, knocking
on the door, calling for him to wake up, come outside.

He appears at last, groggy with sleep.

                              LARRY
          What's so important?

                    MORRIS
          Record company called! They want to
          hear our music in the studio.

                    LARRY
          They called you?

                    DARRYL
          They called me. They said they tried
          you. You never called back.

                    LARRY
          If they called, I'm pretty sure I
          would remember.

                    DARRYL
          Dig, like we got the call, it's
          alright. We need to move before
          they might change their minds. Let's
          go.

                    LARRY
          Oh, you Mister Show Business now?
          This isn't professional! Call at
          business hour - not three in the
          morning!!

                    DARRYL
          It's a record company, they don't
          keep bankers' hours. Come on.

Larry closes the door on them.

INT. LARRY'S HOUSE

He leans against the door, gathering himself all over again.
Okay. Here we go.

INT. RECORD COMPANY HEADQUARTERS - NIGHT

HALLWAY:

The Dramatics wait their turn to audition, standing around
in the outer hallway, from which they can see a little bit
inside the glass studio where -

INT. STUDIO

Seated around the studio are a group of jazz session
musicians, studio pros who've seen it all, done it all.

They are ushered into the room.

The Dramatics gawk at the grizzled pros and the assembly of
shiny equipment.

Impatient behind the glass partition, HARRY, the hard-driving
impresario, clicks the mic -

                    HARRY
               (over mic)
          You guys had better be good because
          I'm broke.

Larry hesitates - or did he freeze up - Morris steps up to
the mic.

                    MORRIS
          Yes, sir. One, two, One, two three
          four - and -

The singing starts.

Very quickly realize that Larry is only lip-syncing.

The song sounds thin.

Morris shoots him a look, raised eyebrows.

                    MORRIS (CONT'D)
               (to the boss)
          Excuse me, Sir. Can we have a minute?

EXT. STREET - LATER

Larry paces. Morris goes right at him.

                    MORRIS
          What's in your head? You were lip-
          syncing.

                    LARRY
          How am I supposed to sing with what
          happened to Fred?

                    MORRIS
          You just do it.

                    LARRY
          Sing 'Dancing in the Streets' when
          my boy is lying dead. Come on.

                    MORRIS
          A song is not words on a page. That's
          not music. Music is what you put
          into it. You can make that whatever
          you want.

                    LARRY
          I'm not singing for Motown so white
          motherfuckers can dance.

                    MORRIS
          They ain't dancing for free.

Larry walks away -

                    MORRIS (CONT'D)
                 (to his back)
          Since when do you care if white people
          dance?

Then Morris realizes how much his friend has changed.

                                                    CUT TO:

EXT. DETROIT BLACK NEIGHBORHOOD - MONTHS LATER

A MAILMAN stands in front of a house looking for a mailbox.

A YOUNG BLACK GIRL stares at him from a stoop.

                    YOUNG BLACK GIRL
          Who you got mail for?

                    MAILMAN
          Cleveland Larry Reed.

The YOUNG BLACK GIRL walks down, sticks out her hand.

                    YOUNG BLACK GIRL
          I'll take it to him.

He hands her the envelope. We follow her back inside as she
passes through the entryway -

INT. HOUSE - CONTINUOUS

- Past a living room crowded with RELATIVES -

- Through the living room - and up the stairs -

                    YOUNG BLACK GIRL
                 (shouting upstairs)
          LARRY! You got a letter!
                 (she looks at it)
          From the government!

An OLDER WOMAN appears at the top of the stairs. Takes the
letter from the YOUNG BLACK GIRL.

                    OLDER WOMAN
          I'll give it to him.

We follow the OLD WOMAN now, staying with the letter, as she walks down the hall, where we see various BOARDERS in the rooms.

She gets to the end of the hall - KNOCKS ON THE DOOR - gets no answer.

She opens it.

Sees Larry lying on the bed. He gives no answer. She kneels down next to him and hands him the letter.

He opens it.

Something official from a court, and a BUS TICKET.

                                              CUT TO:

EXT. BUS STATION - AFTERNOON

Larry stands in line for a bus upstate.

                                              CUT TO:

INT./EXT. BUS

LARRY is on the BUS, staring out the window.

He's never seen so much greenery in his life.

Everyone else on the bus is white.

                                              CUT TO:

EXT. BUS - MUCH LATER

The bus pulls up in a small SUBURBAN TOWN and -

LARRY STEPS OUT, looks around, lost.

Unfriendly stares from workers nearby.

                    LARRY
          Excuse me. Which way is the
          courthouse?

The WORKERS snort. *Naturally, he's looking for the courthouse.*

                                              CUT TO:

EXT. COURTHOUSE - LATER

Larry climbs the front steps.

INT. RECORDERS COURT, COURTHOUSE - CONTINUOUS

Larry enters and sees way at the front, past the rows and
rows of white people, a small pocket of black men and women.

                                                      CUT TO:

INT. RECORDERS COURT - LATER

AUERBACH, the confident defense attorney, talks very fast to
Roberts, the member of the National Guard, who is now on the
witness stand.

                    AUERBACH
          You saw the flash before you heard
          the gun shot. Is that your testimony?

Larry watches from the audience.

                    ROBERTS
          I can't say for sure -

His questions come raining down before Roberts is finished.

                    AUERBACH
          Well which is it? Which came first.
          Did you see the flash?

                    ROBERTS
          It is pretty confusing -

                    AUERBACH
          - Well, now, you said before that
          you might be confused, that you didn't
          know what point of time these things
          happened. Are you confused?

                    ROBERTS
          Yes, sir.

                    AUERBACH
          Thank you.

                    ROBERTS
          I can't -

                    AUERBACH
          - Thank you -

                                                      CUT TO:

INT. COURTROOM - LATER

Everyone is in the same position, but a new witness is on
the stand, Greene.

104

                    AUERBACH
Being a military man you would be
able to distinguish between the
uniforms of a National Guardsman
with that of a Detroit Police officer,
is that correct?

                    GREENE
I suppose.

                    AUERBACH
And so you say that the man that
took the victim, Mr. Pollard, into
the room, that he was a National
Guardsman and so I presume that you
know this because he was wearing a
uniform of the National Guard.

                    GREENE
Yes, I saw a guy in uniform take him
back there.

                    AUERBACH
Did you see anybody else go back
into that room?

                    GREENE
No.

                    AUERBACH
Would you have been able to see
anybody else go back into that room,
at that time, wasn't your head turned
back by the police officers who were
still standing there with you?

                    GREENE
Yes.

                    AUERBACH
Yes what? How could you see if
anybody else was taken back into
that room if your head was turned
subsequent to the man you say was in
a uniform.

                    GREENE
I couldn't see after that.

                    AUERBACH
So for all you know, any number of
people could have gone into that
room. Or left for that matter.
                    (MORE)

                    AUERBACH (CONT'D)
          And in fact, you can't say for certain
          who was in the room at all. The man
          in the uniform could have walked
          directly out, couldn't he have?

                                             CUT TO:

INT. COURTROOM - MORNING

                    AUERBACH
          And so in the lineup when you were
          asked to identify the officers who
          beat you, who did you identify? Do
          you see him here in court today?

                    KAREN
          Him and him.
               (pointing to Krauss
                and Flynn)

                    AUERBACH
          But you have just identified both of
          the defendants. Why did you not
          identify both of them at the time in
          the lineup? Why did you only identify
          one of them if they both took part
          in beating you? Which recollection
          for the record, would you say is the
          correct recollection?

                    KAREN
          I just said...I couldn't tell at
          first. When I went down to the police
          station, I was very nervous.

                    AUERBACH
          So now you are calm and you will not
          be changing your story, again , then?
          This is it? This is the one you
          want us to work with?

                                             CUT TO:

INT. COURTROOM - LATER

                    AUERBACH
          Isn't it a fact, Mr. Reed, that
          your head was against the wall for
          most of the evening.

                    LARRY
          My hands were on the wall, that's
          a fact.

                    AUERBACH
          I asked about your head.

                    LARRY
          My head is attached to my neck. It
          moves -
               (he moves his head to
                demonstrate)
          This way and that.

                    AUERBACH
          And yet it cannot turn completely
          around to see what's behind you, or
          do have a special skill the courtroom
          should know about?

                                             CUT TO:

INT. COURTROOM LATER - MORNING

                    LEE
          He put me down on the floor and then
          he fired a shot and told me to keep
          my mouth shut and lay still or the
          next one would be for real.

                    AUERBACH
          And what did you do?

                    LEE
          I lay still.

                    AUERBACH
          And were you mistreated, in any way,
          after that.

                    LEE
          Mistreated?

                    AUERBACH
          Have you ever been arrested, sir.

                    LEE
          Sure.

                    AUERBACH
          Ever spent a night in jail.

                    LEE
          Sure.

                    AUERBACH
          How many times have you been arrested
          and how many nights and days have
                    (MORE)

                                                         107

                    AUERBACH (CONT'D)
          You spent in prison for crimes you
          committed or alleged to have
          committed? Criminal acts, that is.

                                              CUT TO:

INT. COURTROOM - LATER

                    AUERBACH
          Thank you.
               (to the judge)
          Next witness, your honor.

                                              CUT TO:

INT. RECORDER'S COURT - LATER

The JUDGE, DEFENSE TEAM and PROSECUTION are considering the
merits of omitting the police confessions. Both lawyers
stand before the JUDGE.

All the following is said very quickly, with an almost rote
mechanical quality that underscores the mind-numbing nature
of a legal loop hole:

                    LANG
          If your honor pleases. These were
          police officers sophisticated in the
          knowledge of their constitutional
          rights, having been trained in this.

                    AUERBACH
          I think what is crystal clear here,
          Your Honor, is that these men were
          under an intolerable situation.
          They were under this duress, which
          we say is inherent, and for that
          reason they had no other choice.

                    LANG
          Alright. All they had to do was
          keep quiet. If they kept quiet,
          they wouldn't be here today.
          But they didn't. They made a
          statement, and that statement should
          be admissible.

                    AUERBACH
          Not if it was made under duress,
          Your Honor. Not if the taking of
          the statement violates constitutional
          rights.

108

                              JUDGE
               These policemen were owed an
               obligation, the same obligation owed
               to any citizen, advising them that
               they had a right to remain silent,
               they had a right to consult, and
               anything that they said could be
               used against them in a court of law.
               That would be so if there was any
               other person, any regular, ordinary
               citizen. The police would have to
               advise an ordinary citizen that
               whatever you say can be used against
               you. I don't think these two
               defendants, because they are police
               officers, have any right to expect
               anything more from us, but they have
               a right under the Constitution not
               to settle for anything less. I
               therefore rule the statement
               inadmissible.

In the audience, Conyers can't believe it went this way.

INT. COURTHOUSE HALLWAY - MOMENTS LATER

The hallway is massively overcrowded, defendants huddling in
one corner, surrounded by UNIFORMED POLICE OFFICERS. Victims
in the other corner. They start filing back inside the
courtroom.

EXT. COURTHOUSE ALLEY - MOMENTS LATER

All the defendants - Krauss, Flynn, Demens and Dismukes are
taking a quick break away from the attorneys, gathered around
an ashtray, smoking.

                              KRAUSS
                         (to Dismukes)
               Isn't this just a load of bullshit?

                              DISMUKES
               You know as well as I do those kids
               shouldn't have been killed like that.

                              KRAUSS
               Yeah, shame. They resisted. They
               should have complied with a lawful
               order to relinquish their weapons.

Krauss slaps him on the shoulder

                              KRAUSS (CONT'D)
               You're a solid guy.

                              DISMUKES
                    Excuse me.

Dismukes walks away from the group and we follow him into
the parking lot -

EXT. PARKING LOT

Dismukes walks stiffly to a private spot, trying to gather
himself and then his body can't keep the contradictions buried
any longer and he finds himself doubled over puking -

Vomit stains the concrete -

He wipes his mouth and breathes.

EXT. COURTHOUSE - CONTINUOUS

Aubrey's Grandmother, Ma, is outside with a group of
REPORTERS. She's enraged -

                              MA
                    This wouldn't have happened if they
                    found **black** girls in a hotel with
                    white men, no sir. No way would
                    they do this to white men. That's
                    the truth and I don't care who knows
                    it. They can't shut me up, no sir.

                              REPORTER
                    Thank you, M'am. How does it feel
                    to have lost your Grandson?

Maw shoots him a look. Can this guy be serious?

                              MA
                         (sincerely)
                    It's a terrible pain. It never goes
                    away.

John Conyer pulls her away from the press vultures.

                              CONYERS
                         (to the reporter)
                    Why don't you conduct yourself with
                    a little empathy. We're here today
                    to witness the Justice System at
                    work - and we demand that police
                    criminality be treated the same as
                    any other kind of criminality.

                              REPORTER
                    Some people would say it's wrong to
                    judge police for doing their jobs.

                              CONYERS
                    Nice try. You have my comment.
                       (spelling it out)
                    Police criminality needs to be treated
                    the same as any other kind of
                    criminality.

INT. COURTHOUSE - CONTINUOUS

There's a moment where Larry almost crosses paths with Krauss,
as they're both heading into the courtroom at the same time.
Krauss lets him go first.

INT. COURTROOM - LATER

Everyone is seated. Waiting for the jury to come back.

The JURY MEMBERS shuffle back into the room.

We pan across their faces - all white.

                              JUDGE
                       (to JURY)
                    Has the jury reached a decision in
                    this matter, with regards to the
                    charges of murder in the first degree
                    and assault?

                              HEAD JUROR
                    We have, your honor.

                              JUDGE
                    Well, would you like to tell the
                    court what it is?

VERY TIGHT ON THE HEAD JUROR'S FACE:

                              HEAD JUROR
                    On the assault, not guilty. As to
                    the murder charges ... not guilty.

                                                       CUT TO:

BRIGHT NEON LIGHTS OF THE FOX THEATER MARQUEE:

THE DRAMATICS!

EXT. FOX THEATER

A crowd buys tickets to the show.

INT. FOX THEATER

The DRAMATICS are on stage in full performance mode.

Twist, turn and smile.

                    MORRIS
                  (signing)
            I'm as real as real can be,
            What you see is what you get

We clock the boys, one by one. Someone is missing.

CROWD:

Everyone enjoying the show, except for Larry.

Never thought he'd be in the audience.

STAGE:

The boys are dazzling.

EXT. FOX THEATER - LATER

The Dramatics shuffle out of the stage door, passing Larry
who is leaning on the side of the building. They almost
don't notice him until Larry grabs Morris' elbow. The band
stops - unsure of what to say to Larry.

                    MORRIS
                  (to the rest of the
                   group)
            Ya'll go on ahead.

Inside Larry, the betrayal boils over -

                    LARRY
            This is my group.

                    MORRIS
            We got a contract. Nothing you can
            say.

                    LARRY
            Come on, you leave me like this?

                    MORRIS
            Can I try to talk to you for a minute?

                    LARRY
            ...

                    MORRIS
          If something is good, it's good no
          matter what. Even if you kill it.
          See what I'm saying?

Larry doesn't.

                    MORRIS (CONT'D)
          Fred will always be good. They can't
          take that.

                    LARRY
          I hear you.

                    MORRIS
          Okay then. We gotta snatch this
          opportunity.

                    LARRY
          Not like this.

                    MORRIS
          Man, Motown is a black-owned company.

                    LARRY
          You know what I mean. Who listens
          to this *music*. It's not easy for
          me.

                    MORRIS
          We all a long way from easy.

What more is there to say.

They clasp hands, hug.

Genuine warmth.

                    LARRY
          You do what you need. I'm gonna lay
          low.

Morris turns back to join the waiting band.

                                        CUT TO:

EXT. DETROIT - WINTER - MONTHS LATER

A heavy snowfall blankets the wrecked city.

Larry trudges through the icy muck, jacket wrapped against
the cold.

A deflated man.

INT. LARRY'S APARTMENT - LATER

It is damn small. Stove going - water on the boil - but not
much to eat. Larry opens the cupboard and shakes a box of
rice. Empty.

He goes for some beans.

EXT. DETROIT STREET - SOUTHERN BAPTIST CHURCH

Larry stands outside the Church, thinking.

INT. CHURCH - MOMENT LATER

He walks around and finds the Pastor in the back, writing a
sermon.

                    LARRY
          Excuse me, brother.

The Pastor looks up.

                    LARRY (CONT'D)
          I submitted an application for the
          Church Choir Director and never heard
          back. Larry Reed?

                    PASTOR
          I remember. From the Dramatics,
          right? As I recall you were
          overqualified as a professional
          musician. We're just a neighborhood
          church.

                    LARRY
          I am overqualified. So?

                    PASTOR
          Well, why don't you go try some of
          the clubs downtown, I'm sure they'd
          be happy to have you and I can
          guarantee you the pay will be better.

                    LARRY
          Lotta police in those you clubs, you
          know, it's dangerous. Can you help?
          I need a job.

                    PASTOR
          I think I understand.

EXT. CHURCH - LATER

Larry stands outside the Church, then heads home.

We follow him as he walks, turns a corner, and passes by the Fox Theater.

He doesn't look up at the marquee.

CUT TO:

INT. CHURCH - CHOIR PRACTICE ROOM

Larry Reed at a piano in a modest practice room. He is surrounded by an eclectic mix of BLACK LADIES on folding chairs, who are fanning themselves, waiting for him to play.

Larry is very nervous.

He hasn't approached a piano since the Algiers murders.

>   LARRY
>   Alright, I'm not gonna lie. It's
>   been awhile.

He wipes his sweaty hands.

>   LARRY (CONT'D)
>   Well, let's see what you got. Ready?
>   And ah- One, two three -

He strikes the keys -

CUT TO:

BLACK

Then back to Larry.

He plays with real grace and fluidity. A natural.

The CHOIR begins.

Larry joins in.

His voice, which we haven't heard in forever, is loud and clear.

And getting stronger.

As he sings, these TITLES:

AT LEAST 41 CIVILIANS AND ONE POLICE OFFICER WERE KILLED DURING THE DETROIT UNREST.

NO LAW ENFORCEMENT OFFICIALS WERE EVER CONVICTED FOR THE KILLINGS.

YEARS LATER, A CIVIL COURT RULED AGAINST ONE OF THE OFFICERS PRESENT AT THE ALGIERS HOTEL MURDERS.

HE WAS ORDERED TO PAY A FINE OF $5,000.

THE DRAMATICS BROKE OUT IN THE 1970s, WITH SEVERAL HIT SINGLES ON THE MOTOWN CHARTS.

THE GROUP CONTINUES TO PERFORM TO THIS DAY.

CLEVELAND LARRY REED STILL LIVES IN DETROIT.